S0-AIP-346

SECRET
SINGAPORE

Heidi Sarna
and Jerome Lim

JONGLEZ PUBLISHING

travel guides

O'Neal Library
50 Oak Street
Mountain Brook, AL
35213

Writer Heidi Sarna has lived in Singapore for over 15 years and she started exploring soon after she arrived, eager to uncover the secrets behind the island's shiny modern office and apartment towers. Her journey of discovery started with her finding the ruins of an abandoned colonial-era house that had been swallowed up by the relentless tropical sprawl. When she's not nosing around Singapore's back lanes and forgotten places, Heidi writes about travel and small-ship adventure cruising for her award-winning blog, QuirkyCruise.com, which earned an Honorable Mention in the SATW Foundation Lowell Thomas Travel Journalism Competition 2018–2019.

Singaporean heritage enthusiast Jerome Lim has been writing the 'The Long and Winding Road' blog since 2008 as a repository for his memories of old Singapore. Considered one of the most knowledgeable authorities on the island's history, Jerome loves exploring and photographing the Singapore many people have forgotten or never knew existed. A naval architect by profession, he also leads tours to offbeat places for the Singapore Land Authority (SLA). JeromeLim loves nothing better than researching fascinating aspects of Singapore's past in the National Library or out in the field, notebook and camera in hand, searching for vestiges of what has come before.

We have taken great pleasure in drawing up *Secret Singapore* and hope that through its guidance you will, like us, continue to discover unusual, hidden or little-known aspects of the city-state.

Descriptions of certain places are accompanied by thematic sections highlighting historical details or anecdotes as an aid to understanding the city-state in all its complexity. *Secret Singapore* also draws attention to the multitude of details found in places that we may pass every day without noticing. These are an invitation to look more closely at the urban landscape and, more generally, a means of seeing our own city with the curiosity and attention that we often display while travelling elsewhere ...

Comments on this guidebook and its contents, as well as information on places we may not have mentioned, are more than welcome and will enrich future editions.

Don't hesitate to contact us:
E-mail: info@jonglezpublishing.com
Jonglez Publishing, 25 rue du Maréchal Foch
78000 Versailles, France

Johor Bahru
(Malaysia)

Sembawang

Woodlands

Lim
Chu Kang

Choa
Chu Kang

Bukit
Panjang

Central
Catchment
Nature Reserve

SINGAPORE

Bukit
Batok

Iskandar
Puteri

Boon Lay

Tuas

Jurong
West

Jurong
East

Bukit
Timah

p. 136

Clementi

Jurong Island

Alexandra

Busing

Bukom

Sudong

Sebarok

Pawai

Semakau

Senang

N

0   5   10 km

p. 154

Simpang

Pasir Gudang

Yishun

Seletar

Ubin

Punggol

Thomson

Sengkang

Hougang

Pasir Ris

Loyang

Bishan

Tampines

✈ **Changi Airport**

Potong
Pasir

Simei

Bedok

p. 108

Geylang

Little
India

Tanjong
Katong

Fort
Canning

p. 46

Tanjong
Pagar

p. 10

Brani

Sentosa

Singapore Strait

Batam
(Indonesia)

p. 204

CONTENTS

Chinatown and Tanjong Pagar

JAMES CUTLER MAIL CHUTE	*12*
STRAITS SETTLEMENTS POLICE CREST	*14*
BASKETBALL-THEMED WINDOW GRILLS	*16*
SINGAPORE CITY GALLERY	*18*
SINGAPORE LAND INDENTURES	*20*
SINGAPORE'S OLDEST LIFT	*21*
THE VIEW FROM PINNACLE@DUXTON	*24*
THE HEXAGONAL PAVILION OF THE TIGER BALM PAGODA	*26*
DUXTON PLAIN PARK	*28*
NUS BABA HOUSE	*30*
THE FAÇADE OF 66 SPOTTISWOODE PARK ROAD	*32*
MEMORIAL AND SHRINE TO SIKH MARTYR BHAI MAHARAJ SINGH	*34*
TANAH KUBUR DIRAJA	*36*
SINGAPORE GENERAL HOSPITAL MUSEUM	*38*
SECRETS OF THE "HOME" MURAL	*40*
CIVILIAN PRE-WAR AIR-RAID SHELTER	*42*
TAN TOCK SENG'S TOMBSTONE	*44*

Fort Canning and the Civic District

FULLERTON HOTEL HERITAGE GALLERY	*48*
THE EARLY FOUNDERS' STONE	*50*
THE PLAQUE OF ANDERSON BRIDGE	*52*
TAN KIM SENG FOUNTAIN	*54*
REMAINS OF STAMFORD BRIDGE	*56*
THE FOOT OF THE SIR STAMFORD RAFFLES STATUE	*58*
TUDOR ROSE	*60*
BRONZE THAI ELEPHANT	*62*
CITY HALL CHAMBER	*64*
LIONS ON THE ELGIN BRIDGE	*66*
PHANTOM POOL	*68*
FORT CANNING LIGHTHOUSE	*70*

FREEMASONS HALL	*72*
SARKIES PHANTOM TOMBS	*74*
MEMORIAL TO JAMES BROOKE NAPIER	*76*
TOMBSTONE WALL	*78*
THE MACE OF SINGAPORE	*80*
A PAUL REVERE BELL	*82*
THE SINGAPORE STONE	*84*
DRINKING FOUNTAIN AT THE NATIONAL MUSEUM OF SINGAPORE	*86*
OLD LIBRARY GATE PILLARS	*88*
THE ORGAN OF THE CATHEDRAL OF THE GOOD SHEPHERD	*90*
BABY GATE OR THE GATE OF HOPE	*92*
STAINED GLASS WINDOWS AT JACOB BALLAS CENTRE	*94*
EX MALAYAN MOTORS SHOWROOM	*96*
MANASSEH MEYER'S INITIALS	*98*
SHOPHOUSE AT NO.1 TANK ROAD	*100*
GATE PILLARS OF NAN CHIAU HIGH SCHOOL	*102*
CHEE GUAN CHIANG HOUSE	*104*
THE COLONNADE	*106*

Selegie Road, Little India and Kampong Glam

BUILDINGS OF MIDDLE ROAD'S EARLY COMMUNITIES	*110*
ELLISON BUILDING'S CUPOLAS	*114*
THE SUNBURST OF MASJID ABDUL GAFFOOR	*116*
GODDESS KALI WITH A BITE	*118*
NIGHT SOIL VENTS	*120*
ORIGINAL GATE TO "THE NEW WORLD" AMUSEMENT PARK	*122*
PETAIN ROAD TOWNHOUSES	*124*
JALAN KUBOR CEMETERY	*126*
ZUBIR SAID'S PIANO	*128*
THE SOY SAUCE BOTTLE BOTTOMS OF THE SULTAN MOSQUE	*130*
THE LEANING MINARET OF HAJJAH FATIMAH MOSQUE	*132*
GASHOLDER FRAME	*134*

CONTENTS

Botanic Gardens and Environs

ISTANA WOODNEUK	138
LIBRARY OF BOTANY AND HORTICULTURE	140
SINGAPORE BOTANIC GARDENS' TIGER ORCHID	141
ARROWS ON BRICKS	142
GIRL ON A SWING SCULPTURE	144
THE FLAGPOLE OF "EDEN HALL"	146
A STUMP-UMENT TO SINGAPORE'S FIRST RUBBER TREE	148
WOODEN ARROW	150
WWII POW CALENDAR	152

Bukit Timah, Southern Coast, Jurong and North

THE PIER AT LIM CHU KANG	156
WOODLANDS JETTY	158
KAMPUNG ADMIRALTY ROOFTOP	160
SEMBAWANG HOT SPRINGS	162
SYONAN JINJA SHRINE	164
BUKIT TIMAH SUMMIT	166
BOARDROOM AT THE FORMER FORD FACTORY	168
LITTLE GUILIN	170
NANTAH ARCH	172
GARDEN OF FAME	174
MACHINE-GUN PILLBOX	176
THE ORIGINAL STEPS TO HAW PAR VILLA	178
THE GAP	180
YING FO FUI KUN CEMETERY	182
THE PLAQUE OF ALEXANDRA HOSPITAL	184
FORMER BREWMASTER'S HOUSE	186
FULLERTON HOTEL LIGHTHOUSE BEACON	188
WHITE OBELISK AT LABRADOR PARK	190
A WARTIME JAPANESE GRAVE	192

HARBOURFRONT 19TH-CENTURY STEAM CRANE   194

FORT IMBIAH BATTERY   196

SENTOSA BOARDWALK   198

THE TOWERS OF LIGHTS SEEN FROM GHOST ISLAND   200

RAFFLES LIGHTHOUSE   202

The Heartland, East Coast and Changi

ONE-TWO-SIX CAIRNHILL ARTS CENTRE   206

THE BLACK AND WHITE HOUSES AT MOUNTPLEASANT ROAD   208

THE SIKH TOMB GUARDIANS OF BUKIT BROWN CEMETERY   210

BUKIT BROWN CEMETERY PEACOCK TILES   212

BLOCK 53 TOA PAYOH'S Y SHAPE   214

JAPANESE CEMETERY PARK   215

FIRST POSTWAR FILM STUDIO   216

OLD KHONG GUAN BISCUIT FACTORY   218

KALLANG AIRPORT RUNWAY   220

OLD SEAWALLS   222

TOK LASAM'S GRAVE   224

JACKIE CHAN'S ANCIENT CHINESE HOUSES   226

RETRO TV TEST PATTERN MURALS   228

OLD CHANGI PRISON GATES   230

THE FACES OF CHANGI MURALS   232

THE JOHORE BATTERY   234

CHANGI BEACH MASSACRE MARKER   236

TECK SENG'S PLACE   238

STATUE OF THE BLESSED VIRGIN MARY   240

KAMPONG LORONG BUANGKOK   242

KAYAKING ON SUNGEI KHATIB BONGSU RIVER   246

ADMIRALTY HOUSE BOMB SHELTER   248

BEAULIEU HOUSE   250

ALPHABETICAL INDEX   252

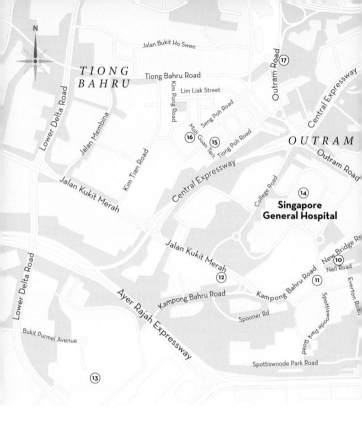

Chinatown and Tanjong Pagar

1. JAMES CUTLER MAIL CHUTE — *12*
2. STRAITS SETTLEMENTS POLICE CREST — *14*
3. BASKETBALL-THEMED WINDOW GRILLS — *16*
4. SINGAPORE CITY GALLERY — *18*
5. SINGAPORE LAND INDENTURES — *20*
6. SINGAPORE'S OLDEST LIFT — *21*
7. THE VIEW FROM PINNACLE@DUXTON — *24*
8. THE HEXAGONAL PAVILION OF THE TIGER BALM PAGODA — *26*
9. DUXTON PLAIN PARK — *28*

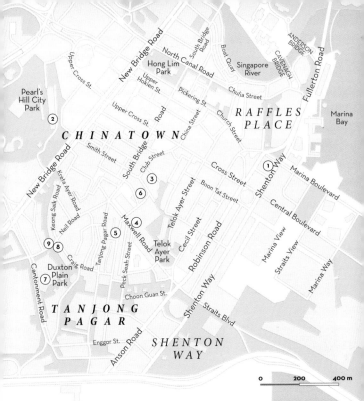

⑩ NUS BABA HOUSE   *30*

⑪ THE FAÇADE OF 66 SPOTTISWOODE PARK ROAD   *32*

⑫ MEMORIAL AND SHRINE TO SIKH MARTYR BHAI

    MAHARAJ SINGH   *34*

⑬ TANAH KUBUR DIRAJA   *36*

⑭ SINGAPORE GENERAL HOSPITAL MUSEUM   *38*

⑮ SECRETS OF THE "HOME" MURAL   *40*

⑯ CIVILIAN PRE-WAR AIR-RAID SHELTER   *42*

⑰ TAN TOCK SENG'S TOMBSTONE   *44*

JAMES CUTLER MAIL CHUTE

An unusual system invented in 1883

Ascott Raffles Place
2 Finlayson Green
MRT: Raffles Place

More commonly found in an early New York City skyscraper, a classic old James Cutler mail chute fits right in at its home in the old-world 18-story Art Deco-influenced Ascott Raffles Place, originally the Asia Insurance Building, on Finlayson Green.

Clad in some 20,000 cream-colored travertine tiles, the edifice is a breath of fresh air in the financial district's chaos of glass and steel and its interiors are impressively well-preserved. A fine example of Singapore's progressive architectural scene of the 1950s – its designer, Ng Keng Siang, was a pioneering local architect – the building holds the distinction of being the first earthquake-proof building in Southeast Asia and was, at its completion in 1955, the region's tallest building.

The Ascott's mail chute, which is finished in brass, allows mail to be deposited from 15 of the building's floors. A notice posted on each floor provides instructions for use. Letters, which the notice advises should be dropped one at a time, should also not be folded. Large or bulky items were also not to be deposited. A "receiving box" on the building's first floor is where the mail ends up, most of the time that is. A number of undelivered items (personal letters, greeting cards and invoices accumulated over the years) were discovered, stuck in the chute, during the building's revamp in the 2000s, when the building was transformed into a block of luxury serviced-residences.

Invented by James Goold Cutler in 1883, the chute seemed an essential addition to the towering structures changing the face of America's cities at the turn of the 20th century. Cutler, an architect from the city of Rochester, New York, and the city's one-time mayor, held a patent for the design and supplied some 1,600 such chutes during the patent's two-decade term. The chute designs also found their way outside the U.S. and fell out of favor due to the many instances of mail being stuck. One of its later installations, the chute at the Asia Insurance Building – as with those installed in New York City and other American cities – was in one of the buildings that was to herald the then municipality's own 'age of the skyscraper'.

STRAITS SETTLEMENTS POLICE CREST

A crest that was used on the badge of the Straits Settlements police uniform

Pearl's Hill Upper Barracks
195 Pearl's Hill Terrace, Singapore 168976
MRT: Chinatown or Outram

Very easy to overlook, the molded crest above the central entrance of Pearl's Hill Upper Barracks speaks of an era in Singapore's history. Comprised of three crowns inside a red diamond shape above the words "Straits Settlements Police," it's the image that was used on the badge of the Straits Settlements police uniform. The three crowns represent the three settlements of Singapore, Malacca and Penang (once known as Prince of Wales Island).

The imposing Upper Barracks building is perched on the southern slopes of Pearl's Hill, one of the highest spots in the city center and for a large part of the 20th century, an important vantage point for watching over Chinatown and much of Singapore.

Built by the Public Works Department in simplified Neo-Classical style in 1934, it is of a length that would have placed it among the longest civic structures of the era. In more recent years, it was used to house Government Ministries involved with security and also the Police headquarters. Clues to the building's original purpose – as police barrack accommodation – lie in its name, the building's design, and that rather nondescript crest. The building's airy corridors and courtyards, allowing a maximum of natural light and ventilation, are hallmarks of British tropical barrack designs. Its scale is an indication of the sizeable contingent it housed – the huge Sikh Contingent.

With a reputation for fearlessness and discipline, many Sikhs were recruited by the British for the military and the police. The police reorganization program of the late 1920s brought many more Sikhs to Singapore from India. New barracks were needed and so the Upper Barracks was built for married policemen and their families and a Lower Barracks for the unmarried. With the disbanding of the Sikh Contingent after the war, the Upper and Lower Barracks housed the Police Radio Division. Following independence in 1965, the Upper Barracks became the Ministry of Interior and Defence. In 1970, that was split into the Ministry of Defence and the Ministry of Home Affairs, which continued using the Upper Barracks until 1977. The building was then used as the Police Headquarters until 2001.

Pearl's Hill is a reminder of James Pearl, captain of the *Indiana* – the ship that carried Sir Stamford Raffles to Singapore at its founding. Pearl purchased it in 1822 with the intention to cultivate pepper. Over the years, it has hosted a Chinese Pauper's Hospital – the predecessor to Tan Tock Seng Hospital – as well as military and police barracks. Outram Prison, demolished in the 1960s, was also placed at the western foot of the hill in the mid-1800s and quarters for wardens were built on the hill.

BASKETBALL-THEMED WINDOW GRILLS

The former clubhouse of the Basketball Association of Singapore

The Goh Loo Club
70 Club Street
MRT: Tanjong Pagar, Chinatown or Telok Ayer

The halls on the first and second level of the Goh Loo Club on Club Street, nondescript as they are in appearance, both have stories to tell. The first level, as can be surmised if you notice the basketball-themed iron window grilles that were added in the 1950s, housed the newly formed Singapore Amateur Basketball Association (SABA), formerly

the Basketball Association of Singapore (BAS), from 1946 to 1971. The association was founded in 1946 by Goh Chye Hin, a basketball enthusiast and president of the Goh Loo Club. The organization helped to popularize basketball in Singapore and sent strong teams to tournaments in the region and even to the Olympics in 1956 in Melbourne, Australia.

The Goh Loo Club on Club Street is one of a handful of exclusive establishments from which the street takes its name. Set up by a group of select Chinese businessmen as a gathering place, its members included Dr. Lim Boon Keng and Lee Kong Chian, both well-respected luminaries of Singapore's past. Founded in 1905, it moved into its current premises in 1927. The clubhouse bears many of the characteristics of the shophouses ubiquitous to Singapore's old urban landscape, with the exception of its unusually large width.

Meeting of the Overseas Chinese Association

Unknown to most, the hall on the second level bore witness to a historically significant event in March 1942, just weeks after Singapore's inglorious capitulation to the Japanese: the inaugural meeting of the Overseas Chinese Association. The formation of the association – at the behest of Mr. Shinozaki, a former press officer sympathetic to the Chinese community – provided a platform for the Chinese community to mediate with the Japanese military authorities who were in the midst of setting in motion one of the worst atrocities of the Occupation: the Sook Ching purge. The purge began less than a week after the fall and saw many in the community rounded up and executed. Some 250 members of the newly-formed association were present, including the elderly Dr. Lim Boon Keng. A $50 million "gift" was demanded to put an end to the purge and as atonement for the local Chinese support of the anti-Japanese movement in China. Despite the odds involved in raising the money, the demand was met following two deadline extensions and required assets to be sold and a loan of $22 million taken from a Japanese bank. The event is also commemorated in a mural on the outside wall of the clubhouse installed in 2016. The faces of some of those present at the meeting, including that of the much-hated General Tomoyuki Yamashita, can be seen in the mural, which also celebrates the members of the working-class Chinese community and more prominent figures such as the revolutionary leader Dr. Sun Yat Sen.

SINGAPORE CITY GALLERY ④

Where Singapore can be seen in miniature

45 Maxwell Rd
Monday–Saturday 9am–5pm
MRT: Chinatown or Tanjong Pagar

To the visitor, Singapore must seem to have had every square inch of its built landscape meticulously planned. While urban planning efforts do not go into such fine detail, a conscious and continuous effort does go into laying out much of Singapore.

The work is undertaken by the Urban Redevelopment Authority (URA) which has captured its efforts in a wonderful 1:400 scale architectural model of Central Singapore inside the rather non-descript looking URA Centre Building, in its Singapore City Gallery.

Found right at the end of the suggested route through the gallery, the model, which represents less than 3 percent of the island, is one of the world's largest. It is also one of the gallery's oldest exhibits, predating its opening, with parts of it built as far back as the early years of Singapore's independence in the late 1960s.

The model is the subject of an hourly light and sound show.

You'll also want to check out the Singapore City Gallery's Islandwide Model, which provides a 1:1000 representation of the whole island of Singapore. It's on the first floor and captures a macro-perspective of Singapore and is constructed of plain balsa wood.

Urban Planning in Singapore involves a long term and integrated approach due to its limited land area. The URA, an agency under the Ministry of National Development, takes the lead in this and involves other government agencies in the Concept Plan that is reviewed every 10 years. The Concept Plan charts land use and transportation over a 40- to 50-year period. A more detailed plan is the Master Plan, which guides development over a 10- to 15-year period. This is reviewed every five years.

SINGAPORE LAND INDENTURES

A window into Singapore's past

Maxwell Reserve Singapore hotel
2 Cook Street
MRT: Maxwell

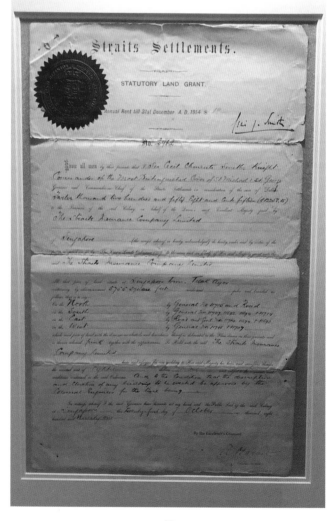

Within the Maxwell Reserve Singapore hotel on Cook Street, few customers pay close attention to the walls of the hotel lobby, full of framed documents. The yellowed papers with hard-to-read calligraphic script are land indentures. These records are a paper trail of the buying and selling of land to establish plantations, build homes and start businesses in colonial-era Singapore and its neighbors in Penang, Malacca, Sarawak and Surabaya.

Shedding light on an era when parts of the region fell under the umbrella of British Malaya, the deeds and transactions refer to Spanish dollars, Indian rupees and Straits dollars, and some are written on behalf of the Queen of England. These currencies were used at various times in Singapore, proving its place as a major trading hub in Southeast Asia over the past two centuries.

The earliest document in the collection is a fragile land indenture from Surabaya in Indonesia dated December 1709. Most of the others are from the 19th century, in the days when the world was mad for tin, rubber and opium. The oldest indentures feature elaborate scripts and ornate adhesive stamps, ink "chops," wax seals and ribbons. Variant spellings reflect the level of schooling or the ethnic background of the clerk who transcribed the document, creating a fascinating tapestry of the customs and conventions of the time.

Some documents are of historical significance because they refer to iconic Singapore locales such as Raffles Place, Serangoon Road, Mount Elizabeth and Beach Road. Others stand out because of the important businessman or statesman represented therein – influential individuals like Thomas Stamford Raffles, Cecil Clementi Smith, Song Ong Siang and Manasseh Meyer, whose legacies carry forward in the names of Singapore roads, bridges and public spaces.

NEARBY
Singapore's oldest lift ⑥
1922-Built Modernist Building
5 Kadayanallur Street

The plain narrow building is Singapore's oldest modernist building and it claims what is thought to be Singapore's oldest working elevator. Designed in 1922 by Harry Robinson of the notable architecture firm Swan & Maclaren, the building was constructed to house St. Andrew's Mission Hospital for Women and Children, serving the poor in neighborhoods in and around nearby Chinatown. The lift, which was retrofitted in 1929, was the only way for patients to access the sunlight and fresh air needed for treatment – on the hospital's rooftop. The Smith, Major & Stevens lift has original wooden panels and collapsible gates. More recently, the building was repurposed for use as offices.

Singapore's land reclamation story: a country that gained 25% of its surface from the sea

Singapore's geology, comprised of a main base of granite with overlying layers of softer sandstone and river sediments, has made it fairly easy to alter Singapore's relatively small size. Its land reclamation story is a fascinating tale of ingenuity and pragmatism: what we see today is vastly different from what anyone would have seen in the early 19th century and before. Land reclamation isn't a recent phenomenon in Singapore. The first project was carried out just three years after Raffles' landing, to build up the southern bank of the Singapore River. Since then, over the course of two centuries, Singapore's land area has increased by some 25 percent, from 58,150 to 71,910 hectares (578 to 719 sq km).

Singapore's Land Growth Over Time

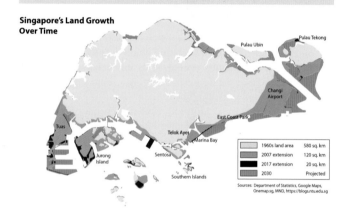

	1960s land area	580 sq. km
	2007 extension	120 sq. km
	2017 extension	20 sq. km
	2030	Projected

Sources: Department of Statistics, Google Maps, Onemap.sg, MND, https://blogs.ntu.edu.sg

The lost islands of Singapore

Singapore is a country comprised of not only the main island of Singapore, but many little islands and islets. Today there are just over 60 islands that make up the republic of Singapore, but there were once at least a dozen more that were removed, filled in or merged with other islands to facilitate land reclamation projects, including Pulau Seking in the south, once as large as 10 football fields, and tiny Pulau Saigon in the Singapore River. Sentosa, formerly known as Pulau Blakang Mati, was formed starting in 1979 by joining a group of islands and so was Jurong Island, which was completed in 2003, by connecting seven islands in the Ayer Chawan archipelago to support Singapore's growing petrochemical industry, adding 3,000 hectares (30 square km) of industrial space.

The lost hills of Singapore

The Singapore of today is a relatively flat isle, with the exception of a few little *bukits* ("hills" in Malay) that pop up across the island. There is the 133-meter-high Bukit Gombak, the 106-meter Bukit Batok, and the 105-meter Mount Faber, to name a few. And there are really just a few. A great number of Singapore's original hills are no longer rolling, having been stripped to supply fill for Singapore's massive ongoing 200-year-long land reclamation efforts.

The first to disappear was a small hill where Battery Road is today. Raffles made the decision to level it. The earth was hauled away by labourers to the marshes along the south side of the Singapore River, where it was used to create Boat Quay.

Shortly after, Chinatown lost Mount Wallich, which was near today's Cecil Street, and Mount Palmer, also known as Parsee Hill, near Tanjong Pagar. Both were blasted out for fill that was needed to extend the shoreline outward from Telok Ayer.

In Chinatown alone there were at least seven hills. Today Pearl's Hill is one of the few survivors, along with Ang Siang Hill and Duxton Hill, none of which are high enough for accolades.

Even Fort Canning Hill wasn't spared, as Straits Settlements Chief Engineer George Collyer lopped off the top to make way for the fort. As recently as the 1970s, hills in Bedok and Tampines were leveled to provide fill for the reclamation of Singapore's East Coast.

Still, the rock and sand blasted and scooped out from flattening Singapore's hills hasn't always been enough, and so sand for building and land reclamation has also been imported from Malaysia, Indonesia, Vietnam and Cambodia. However, recently, many countries are recognizing the environmental harm caused by dredging and exporting such vast amounts of sand, so Singapore has begun innovating to figure out to expand without sand for ongoing reclamation projects in Tuas and other parts of the island.

Malay lexicon

Ayer = Water
Bukit = Hill
Pasir = Beach
Pulau = Island
Sungei = River/estuary
Tanjong = Peninsula

THE VIEW FROM PINNACLE@DUXTON

As impressive as Sands SkyPark atop the Marina Bay Sands

1G Cantonment Road
Daily 9am–9pm
Visitors will need to have an EZ-Link card for access
Get one at MRT stations, 7-Eleven shops or Shell petrol kiosks
MRT: Tanjong Pagar

Topping the tourist bucket list in Singapore is a visit to the observation deck at the Sands SkyPark atop the iconic Marina Bay Sands, but the price of admission is as grand as the view. Few know that there's an equally impressive view to be had not far from Marina Bay, at the top of the Pinnacle@Duxton, the world's tallest public housing building. The cost is four times less.

The complex reaches nearly 537 feet, the exact height of Bukit Timah, Singapore's tallest hill, but because it's in the middle of the city, the views are far better.

From the 50th floor vantage point, visitors can see to the south, the harbor and out to sea where islands belonging to Singapore and Indonesia dot the ocean; to the west, vistas of the Southern Ridges and Mount Faber; to the north, Orchard Road and into the heartlands; and to the east, Chinatown, Shenton Way, the Civic District and Marina Bay.

This is one of the best places to watch the sun set over the city.

Connoisseurs of rooftop vistas can also try ION Sky, on levels 55 and 56 of ION Orchard, to look out over Orchard Road and surrounding neighborhoods.

The world's tallest public housing building

Located near Chinatown on the site of one of the country's first public housing blocks, which were built in 1963 by Singapore's Housing & Development Board (HDB), the Pinnacle@Duxton was completed in 2009. It contains 1,848 individual flats within seven 50-story towers.

The longest continuous sky gardens in the world

The towers of the Pinnacle@Duxton are connected at the 26th and 50th levels by skybridges, which at 1,640 feet each are the longest continuous sky gardens in the world.

Singapore's highest building

Tanjong Pagar Centre, also known as Guoco Tower, stands tall as Singapore's highest building. Measuring in at 951 feet, it bests Bukit Timah, Singapore's highest natural point, by about 414 feet. Completed in 2016, Tanjong Pagar Centre has 64 floors of mixed use space, almost 30 of which are offices.

THE HEXAGONAL PAVILION OF THE TIGER BALM PAGODA

A pavilion that recalls the hexagonal bottles for which Tiger Balm is known

Tiger Balm Building
89 Neil Road
MRT: Outram Park or Chinatown

Neil Road, where Singapore's journey into conservation began, contains many buildings of historical and social significance. One example can be found in a three-story neo-classical-style building angled to fit into the corner of Neil Road's intersection with Craig Road. It was here that Tiger Balm, the Singapore-made herbal medicinal ointment that has found worldwide fame, was once manufactured. Look up to the top of the building to see the six-sided pagoda-like pavilion that represents the little hexagonal bottles for which Tiger Balm is known.

Completed in 1926 at a cost of US$73,530, the building was erected by Aw Boon Haw. Aw found great success in commercializing a formula he inherited from his father, which he initially marketed as "Ten Thousand Golden Oils." Having renamed the balm after himself – his name Boon Haw translates into "gentle tiger" – Aw quickly established himself in the region and set out expanding his business.

A well-respected philanthropist, Aw also founded the Tiger Balm Gardens in Hong Kong and Singapore. Besides the factory, the building housed the offices of Aw's company, Eng Aun Tong, and a "Medical Hall" where the products the factory produced were sold. The factory operated on the premises until 1971 when production was contracted out and a brand new plant was set up for the purpose in Singapore's industrial west. The building received conservation status in 1992.

The Aw brothers

Aw Boon Haw was the driving force behind the Haw Par company that he formed with his younger brother Aw Boon Par. Inheriting his father Aw Chu Kin's company, called Eng Aun Tong, Aw came from Rangoon to Singapore and expanded his reach across the Far East to sell his popular products to Chinese communities in the region. Boon Haw also built Haw Par Villa (see p. 178 "The Original Steps to Haw Par Villa") for his younger brother, who had perished during World War II. Its famed Tiger Balm Gardens were a popular attraction up to the 1970s. Boon Haw was well-known as a benefactor to many social causes. Some of the efforts that benefited from his philanthropy included Boys Town, a trade-school for boys, and The Little Sisters of the Poor, an old-age home.

DUXTON PLAIN PARK

Singapore's oldest railway relic

New Bridge Road to Yan Kit Road
MRT: Outram Park

Close to the heart of busy and congested Chinatown and often overlooked, Duxton Plain Park is a thin green oasis extending from New Bridge Road to Yan Kit Road along a narrow 650-yard corridor. It is cut almost in half at Neil Road, which the park avoids by passing under a bridge. The bridge at Neil Road holds a clue to the park's odd proportions and its lush and fascinating history.

Built for Singapore's first railway to carry vehicular traffic over a 1907 extension to Pasir Panjang, the bridge is now Singapore's oldest railway relic and the only structure left that is connected to the 1903-built Singapore Government Railway. The extension fell into disuse around 1912-14 as did the original line in 1932. Still intact in 1955, the stretch was turned into a public park in 1955. This represents the first instance of a disused railway corridor being preserved for public use – a topic of much public interest these days since Singapore's 15-mile north-south railway corridor was officially closed in 2011. Subsequently the tracks were pulled up and preserving the bed as a green corridor for the public is an ongoing national project.

The bridge also reveals one of the park's main users in its early days, through words in Chinese that read "Chin Woo Athletic Association" seen on a metal frame over one of its sides. The association has its roots in Shanghai and was set up to keep youths out of mischief and away from opium through martial arts training. Its reach spread to Chinese communities outside of China, coming to Singapore in 1922. With its clubhouse at Neil Road, the park made an ideal training site. Its evening lion- and dragon-dance practice sessions would draw scores of curious observers, one of whom was a young assemblyman for the area, the late Lee Kuan Yew. Lee would become Singapore's first and longest serving prime minister and is credited with leading Singapore to where it is today.

Hidden tomb

The southern section of the park runs along the back of the shophouses at Bukit Pasoh, behind one of which a curiously placed tomb – that of a Muslim holy woman by the name of Sharifah Rogaya – can be found. Rather intriguingly, the lone grave sees a string of visitors of other faiths who leave flowers and incense in an act of veneration. A practice with origins in a mystical branch of Islam and frowned upon in the mainstream application of the faith, it is being kept alive by followers outside the faith.

NUS BABA HOUSE

A stunning by-appointment-only museum

157 Neil Road
(65) 6227 5731
babahouse@nus.edu.sg
babahouse.nus.edu.sg
Appointment only
Self-guided visit: Saturday 1:30pm / 2:15pm / 3:15pm / 4pm
Heritage tours (English): Tuesday–Friday 10am
文化遗产导览 *(Mandarin): First Monday of each month 10am*
MRT: Outram Park

By appointment only (there is no sign outside), it is possible to visit the stunning collection of traditional household and personal effects of NUS Baba House, the mansion of a 19th-century tycoon. Painted in a vivid and authentic shade of aquamarine, this old traditional Peranakan (Straits-born Chinese) mansion is a rare pleasure to explore considering how striking and splendidly curated it is.

Those who make the effort are rewarded with a trove of artifacts, many of which belonged to the family of shipping magnate Wee Bin, who purchased the circa 1890s house for his family in 1910. In the 1860s, Wee founded a shipping company that would become one of Singapore's largest Chinese shipping firms by century's end. The house would be occupied by his descendants for decades.

In 2006, it was purchased by the National University of Singapore (NUS) with a donation from Agnes Tan in memory of her late father, renowned Malaysian businessman and community leader Tun Tan Cheng Lock.

The NUS Museum and NUS Department of Architecture teamed up with the Urban Redevelopment Authority (URA) and the Peranakan Association of Singapore to undertake the painstaking task of conservation. It underwent further refurbishment in 2016.

NUS Baba House, named after the title given to Peranakan men, opened two years later. The first two levels are a faithful re-creation of how the Wee family home would have appeared, complete with the family's own mother-of-pearl inlaid blackwood furniture, portraiture, an altar table bearing a shrine, a 2-meter-high Victorian four-poster bed and a tenong, or a wedding gift box. The third level is dedicated to exhibitions highlighting the surrounding neighborhood and community.

Neil Road: a hero of the 1857 Indian Mutiny

Located in the historic Blair Plain district, Neil Road got its name from a hero of the 1857 Indian Mutiny, Colonel Neil of the Madras Fusiliers. Singapore's first prime minister Lee Kuan Yew stayed at 147 Neil Road for a few years of his childhood after it was purchased in 1920 by his grandfather, Lee Hoon Leong. The road is also home to the Jinrikshaw Building, built in 1903, the Eng Tong building where Tiger Balm ointment was manufactured, and for a time, the Fairfield Methodist Girls' School.

THE FAÇADE OF 66 SPOTTISWOODE PARK ROAD

Singapore's oldest surviving painted façade

66 Spottiswoode Park Road
MRT: Outram Park near the Singapore General Hospital

Reliefs and decorative tiles make up much of the embellishments used in a fashion typical of the shophouses built in the early 20th century in Blair Plain, a charming conservation area tucked away on the outer edges of Chinatown, behind the defunct Tanjong Pagar railway station on Keppel Road.

A deviation from this norm is found on the upper façade of a house at 66 Spottiswoode Park Road, on which a decorative fresco is used to

depict archetypally Chinese adornments of flower and animal motifs and auspicious words.

What is less typical is the use of rust-brown and ultramarine blue – a combination that is not very Chinese. Theories postulate that those colors were the only ones available at the time and, further, using fewer colors was cheaper. "Discovered" when layers of coating added over the years faded, the mural is the only one of its kind known to exist in Singapore. Thought to have been painted when the Early Style shophouse on which it's found was built in the 1890s, it also gives the shophouse the distinction of being the one with the oldest painted façade found in Singapore.

The shophouse

Introduced in the 1820s, the shophouse features a combination of Asian and European influences. Shops and other businesses would typically be found on the first floor and living accommodation on the upper levels, when shophouses were used for commercial purposes. Although called a shophouse, many also found use as residences. A key feature seen in many shophouses is the five-foot-way, a sheltered corridor that was the brainchild of Sir Stamford Raffles, modern Singapore's founder. Raffles stipulated this in the 1822 Town Plan, requiring all brick houses to have "a uniform type of front" and "a verandah of a certain depth" to provide "a continuous and covered passage." The idea was thought to have originated from Dutch Batavia during Raffles' time as the Governor of Java, where the architecture was influenced by the verandah-lined buildings of southern Europe's plazas.

Built until the 1960s, shophouses in Singapore come in six distinct styles. The Early style, dating back to the 1840s, is the simplest. The First Transitional style made an introduction in the early 1900s as did the well-decorated Late Style, often referred to as "Chinese Baroque." The less decorated but still dressed Second Transitional style appeared in the 1930s together with those influenced by the Art Deco movement. The Modern style of the 1950s saw a shift towards simplicity and functionality. The shophouses at Blair Plain range from the simple to those that are more elaborately decorated, reflecting not only the status of those who had them built, but also the periods in which they were built.

While many shophouses were demolished during the city's modernization in the 1970s and 1980s, more than 6,000 shophouses have been conserved together with the neighborhoods, such as Blair Plain, in which they are found.

MEMORIAL AND SHRINE TO SIKH MARTYR BHAI MAHARAJ SINGH ⑫

One of the most important figures in Sikh history is buried here

Gurdwara Sahib Silat Road
Silat Road Sikh Temple
8 Jalan Bukit Merah
Daily 5am–9pm
MRT: Outram

Sikhs have been an influential part of Singapore since the port's founding in 1819, even though their numbers have only ever accounted for a small minority of the population. Likewise there are only a handful of Sikh temples in Singapore, which makes it all the more surprising to think that one of the most important figures in Sikh history is buried here, his final resting place a significant memorial for the Sikh community.

Bhai Maharaj Singh was born in 1780 in a village in the Punjab in northwest India. Just 18 years before his birth, an estimated 20,000 to 50,000 Sikhs were massacred by genocidal attacks in repeated Afghan incursions in what is now known as the Second Holocaust or Wadda Ghallughara (the first genocide of the Sikhs happened earlier during the waning years of the Mughal Empire).

Decades later, as the British sought to expand their tentacles further into the subcontinent, they set their sights on annexing the Punjab province and so Bhai Maharaj Singh became a resistance leader, travelling through the province recruiting freedom fighters to his cause. "The Bhai" (or brother), as he was known, led frequent guerilla-style attacks against British cantonments until his arrest in 1849. He was originally interred in India, but the British feared continued unrest as Punjabis increasingly regarded him as a martyr. In 1850 the British decided to move the Bhai and his disciple, who was also jailed, to Singapore, another wing of the British Empire.

At Pearl's Hill Prison, he fell sick with blindness and cancer and died in 1856. The disciple who was transferred with him cremated his remains outside the prison and was later transferred to a different prison in Penang where he, too, died shortly after.

The Bhai was buried within the grounds of the Singapore General Hospital, but after his tombstone became a memorial shrine, it was decided that it would be moved to the nearby gurdwara on Silat Road in 1966. A newer memorial to Bhai Maharaj Singh was built at the gurdwara in 2010, and the shrine continues to attract the devout.

TANAH KUBUR DIRAJA

Royal Cemetery in a public housing estate

Bukit Purmei, near Block 102
MRT: Harbourfront

On a little hillock shrouded in foliage off Kampong Bahru Road, at the edge of a Housing and Development Board (HDB) complex, is the Malay burial ground Tanah Kubur Diraja ('Royal Cemetery'). Also known as Keramat Bukit Kasita, the compound is surrounded by an old thick brick wall and hidden behind the caretaker's wooden dwelling and a cluster of zinc-roofed shacks.

If asked, the chatty caretaker, Umi, welcomes visitors to have a look around. Often sharing what she knows of the compound, she explains that the tombs are those of the Riau-Lingga branch of the Johor royal family and that the oldest grave dates back to 1721, almost a whole century before the British arrived.

It is uncertain when the cemetery was first used. Some accounts date it to the 16th century with links to the descendants and successors of early Singapore's legendary founder, Sang Nila Utama. To other experts, it dates back no later than the early- to mid-19th century. Umi says the Johor royal family owns the cemetery, though a check on the Singapore Land Authority's maps show it within a parcel of land owned by the HDB. It's possible the site itself could still be owned by the Johor State.

Some of the royal headstones are painted yellow or green, and some are covered in yellow cloth (yellow being a royal color and green the color of Islam). Four are richly decorated and sheltered under a tarpaulin held up by metal frames. One of these is believed to be Sultan Iskandar Shah's, an ancestor of the last Sultan of the Johor-Riau-Lingga Empire, Sultan Mahmud III.

SINGAPORE GENERAL HOSPITAL MUSEUM

Intriguing collection of medical artifacts

Bowyer Block
Singapore General Hospital
Third Hospital Avenue
Monday–Friday 9am–6pm, Saturday 9am–1pm
MRT: Outram Park

The old medical equipment in the overlooked Singapore General Hospital Museum is a fascinating feast for anyone drawn to the macabre, from a circa-1900 medical saw that was used for amputations to old vials of arsenic that were once distributed as medicine.

Tucked away in a corner of the sprawling Singapore General Hospital (SGH) complex, this tiny gallery presents an intriguing collection of medical artifacts that are guaranteed to make visitors ponder how their ancestors ever survived early health care: there's an x-ray table from the 1930s, plus old-school stethoscopes including a wooden monoaural stethoscope, urinals and urine test kits, surgical instruments, and obstetric and gynecological equipment. You can have a look at morphine bottles and hypodermic syringes, a blood infusion pump and an old midwife's bag and kit.

To be fair, the displays also champion the heroism of early health care workers and innovators, celebrating Singapore's medical pioneers and some of the hospital's historic firsts, including the first Southeast Asian doctor to have a disease named for him. Tay's Syndrome, discovered by Dr. Tay Chong Hai in 1970, is a rare autosomal recessive disease (when first cousins marry), and is characterized by brittle hair, scaly red skin, prematurely aged faces and bodies, mental abnormalities and sometimes death.

The museum is located in the Bowyer Block, built in 1926 and the only remaining block from the pre-war era. After the war it was named for Dr. John H. Bowyer, chief medical officer of SGH when the Japanese invaded Singapore. He reorganized local hospitals for wartime conditions and served as a civil medical officer at Changi Prison. Sadly, the Japanese tortured him to death after they discovered that he was secretly distributing food to the needy outside the prison. The building was declared a national monument in 2009.

Painted clues to Yip Yew Chong's life

Tiong Bahru
Tiong Poh Rd/Ed Chin St Block 74

Yip Yew Chong is Singapore's most prolific street muralist, covering more and more building walls with his nostalgic feel-good murals. What fans may not realize is that Yew Chong often paints secret little whimsical elements in his works. Just for fun.

His "Home" mural painted in Tiong Bahru in 2016 depicts a classic HDB* living room in 1970s Singapore, complete with the window grills and furniture of the era. Next to a rotary phone, a bottle of Axe oil and a thermos of coffee or tea, a man relaxes in a chair reading the newspaper.

If you look closely at the newspaper, Yew Chong painted former Prime Minister Lee Kuan Yew in an article about Singapore's "speak Mandarin campaign," which was big news in 1979. He also snuck in an article about Lee Kuan Yew's good friend Margaret Thatcher, the former prime minister of the United Kingdom.

Through his art, Yew Chong shares lighthearted clues to his life and the Singapore of yesteryear. He says there are no subversive undertones; what you see is what you get. The details he painted into the "Home"

mural in Tiong Bahru, for instance, were inspired by his uncle's Tiong Bahru home.

*Housing Development Board (HBD) apartments are public housing developments for some 80% of the population

Other secret details

Another mural, "My Chinatown Home" at 30 Smith Street, is a recreation of his childhood home on Sago Lane in Chinatown. Additional elements of Yew Chong's family story are painted into his mural along the back exterior walls of the 19th-century Thian Hock Keng temple at 158 Telok Ayer Street. The massive painting depicts a mix of modern and old Singapore, with both skyscrapers and old-time bumboats setting the scene. It's a lot to take in.

Many don't notice a little girl and an old man painted into the lower left-hand corner. Yew Chong says the girl is his wife as a seven-year-old, the year her father died, and the man is her father as he would look today if he was still alive.

Those in the know will also look for the number 12 that often pops up in Yew Chong's murals on realistically-painted wall calendars, representing the artist's birth date: Jan. 12.

CIVILIAN PRE-WAR AIR-RAID SHELTER

Forgotten air-raid shelter under a public housing estate

Public Housing Complex
Block 78, 41–43 Guan Chuan Street
Guided tours of the air raid shelter are conducted occasionally through various heritage organizations such as the National Heritage Board and licensed tour operators, such as Jane's Singapore Tours
MRT: Tiong Bahru

The hidden civilian pre-war air-raid shelter remained sealed from the world for decades until it was opened for occasional tours in 2012. The World War II-era bomb shelter underneath Block 78 Moh Guan Terrace that once protected Singaporean civilians from Japanese air raids also happened to be the first to have been built below a public housing block.

Unlike most bomb shelters, this one isn't buried deep underground. After entering through a door accessed from the building's outdoor car park, you'll get access to a shelter that covers a cavernous 16,146 square feet, with a capacity for some 1,600 people. Flashlight in hand, you'll see brick walls divide the space into dormitories. Some of the red bricks are marked with "Alexandra Brickworks Company," a local brick maker who at the time had advertised its bricks for building private bomb shelters.

In the mid-1930s, the threat of war in Singapore was unheard of. Still, in 1936 and 1937 a few bomb shelters were built for good measure in Bukit Tunggal at Novena. They were the only ones the government planned to build. However, two years later when war broke out in Europe, those plans changed.

Singaporeans demanded more air-raid shelters, a request that would be difficult and expensive to fulfill in sea-level Singapore, where the ground sits close to the water table. But in 1939 the government relented, and the Singapore Improvement Trust (SIT), which would be replaced by today's Housing and Development Board (HDB), announced a new housing scheme in Tiong Bahru that would have an underground space suitable for a shelter.

It would be built beneath Block 78, the largest of three buildings that made up the "Horse-Shoe Block," named for its unique U shape. A hundred neighborhood residents sought shelter over the weeks leading to Singapore's fall to the Japanese, and just after midnight on January 22, 1942, a baby was born here.

Not exactly Art Deco

Tiong Bahru is known for charming hipster shops and cafes, old-timey coffeeshops and the distinctive architecture of its buildings. But don't call it Art Deco. It's actually in a style called Streamline Moderne, a later stage of Art Deco that stripped away the elaborate ornamentation of the mode, inspired by the simplicity and functionality of the machine age. Tiong Bahru's public housing blocks have curved aerodynamic lines and porthole windows characteristic of airplanes and ocean-liners in the golden age of transportation. The style was popular in public buildings such as airports and railway stations.

TAN TOCK SENG'S TOMBSTONE

Singapore pioneer philanthropist Tan Tock Seng

Outram Road, opposite Shell Petrol station
MRT: Outram Park

Close to the heart of the city, on an overgrown hillock lies the forgotten tomb of the legendary Singapore pioneer philanthropist Tan Tock Seng (1798–1850). The road up the slope to his grave used to lead up to the well-known Chinese Industrial and Commercial Continuation School (better known as 'Kong Shan School'). It was Tan Tock Seng's great-grandson, Tan Kwee Wah (1880–1927), who sold

part of the family burial plot to the school at a discount of 50% in accordance with Tan Tock Seng's philanthropic wishes. The school was demolished in 1988 and the jungle grew up in its place, nearly burying Tan's and a few family members' tombs in tropical foliage.

When Tan Tock Seng died, it's believed he was buried at a cemetery in Pasir Panjang Road. The land where his tomb is now located was acquired by his son, Tan Kim Ching (1829–1892), in 1877 as the family's burial plot. The younger Tan buried his wife, Chua Seah Neo, there when she died in 1882. It was quite possibly at this time that a decision was made to exhume Tan Tock Seng's remains and re-inter them on the same Outram Road site.

From fruit hawker to hospital builder

Tan was born in Malacca and moved to Singapore in 1819 when the British established a trading post here. When he was just 21, Tan started out selling fruits, vegetables and fowl and soon accumulated enough capital to set up shop in Boat Quay. He learned to speak English and got on well with the European traders, going into partnership with John Horrocks Whitehead. It is largely due to their joint speculation in land that Tan became immensely wealthy. Tan's close connections with the local community made him a natural leader and his tact and ability to resolve disputes among the Chinese endeared him to the British, who appointed him the first Asian Justice of the Peace. In 1844, seeing the plight of the indigent on the island, Tan contributed $7,000 towards the construction of a Chinese Pauper's Hospital on top of Pearl's Hill; its mission was to take care of the "diseased of all nations." Construction of the hospital took three years, but after it was completed, it stood empty for two more years due to a lack of funds to equip the hospital and engage staff. In 1849, the first patients were admitted to the hospital and a dozen years later the hospital moved to premises located at the junction of Serangoon and Balestier roads. In 1903, the current site of the hospital, off Moulmein Road, was acquired and the hospital moved once more.

Fort Canning and the Civic District

1. FULLERTON HOTEL HERITAGE GALLERY — 48
2. THE EARLY FOUNDERS' STONE — 50
3. THE PLAQUE OF ANDERSON BRIDGE — 52
4. TAN KIM SENG FOUNTAIN — 54
5. REMAINS OF STAMFORD BRIDGE — 56
6. THE FOOT OF THE SIR STAMFORD RAFFLES STATUE — 58
7. TUDOR ROSE — 60
8. BRONZE THAI ELEPHANT — 62
9. CITY HALL CHAMBER — 64
10. LIONS ON THE ELGIN BRIDGE — 66
11. PHANTOM POOL — 68
12. FORT CANNING LIGHTHOUSE — 70
13. FREEMASONS HALL — 72
14. SARKIES PHANTOM TOMBS — 74
15. MEMORIAL TO JAMES BROOKE NAPIER — 76

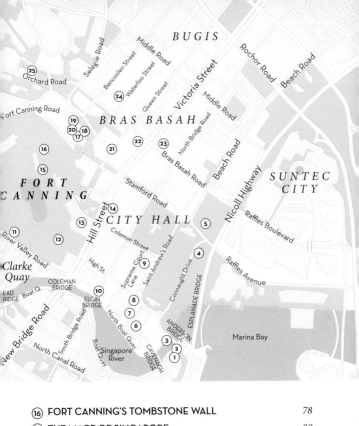

⑯	FORT CANNING'S TOMBSTONE WALL	*78*
⑰	THE MACE OF SINGAPORE	*80*
⑱	A PAUL REVERE BELL	*82*
⑲	THE SINGAPORE STONE	*84*
⑳	DRINKING FOUNTAIN AT THE NATIONAL MUSEUM	
	OF SINGAPORE	*86*
㉑	OLD LIBRARY GATE PILLARS	*88*
㉒	THE ORGAN OF THE CATHEDRAL OF THE GOOD	
	SHEPHERD	*90*
㉓	BABY GATE OR THE GATE OF HOPE	*92*
㉔	STAINED GLASS WINDOWS AT JACOB BALLAS CENTRE	*94*
㉕	EX MALAYAN MOTORS SHOWROOM	*96*
㉖	MANASSEH MEYER'S INITIALS	*98*
㉗	SHOPHOUSE AT NO. 1 TANK ROAD	*100*
㉘	GATE PILLARS OF NAN CHIAU HIGH SCHOOL	*102*
㉙	CHEE GUAN CHIANG HOUSE	*104*
㉚	THE COLONNADE	*106*

FULLERTON HOTEL HERITAGE GALLERY

An unassuming museum in a grand hotel

Fullerton Hotel
1 Fullerton Square
Daily 10am–10pm
MRT: Raffles Place

Overshadowed by Singapore's grander history museums and heritage displays in nearby buildings, the Fullerton Hotel Heritage Gallery is easy to miss within the dramatic hotel's large and impressive lobby. But if you notice it, you'll see it's a treasure chest of artifacts about the Fullerton Building and the surrounding area.

Soak up images of the early maritime waterfront, learn about the economic and political transformations that took place here and bask in nostalgia about the former General Post Office, complete with colonial-era red pillar post box.

When the Fullerton Building was completed in 1928, the General Post Office occupied the first three of its six stories; much of the rest of the building was used by the exclusive European, all-male Singapore Club, a luxurious establishment for the elite, with a 300-foot-long bar.

At the mouth of the Singapore River, the building's location was ideal for receiving and sending post and parcels between ships in the harbor. There was even a tunnel underneath Fullerton Road that had direct, all-weather access to the pier.

The higher floors were occupied by the Ministry of Finance, Department of Trade, Economic Development Board, Monetary Authority of Singapore and Inland Revenue Department, and many a political rally took place in Fullerton Square with the Fullerton Building serving as backdrop.

The Heritage Gallery opened in 2016, celebrating the history of the building and the surrounding area.

In the years that this place served as GPO, it was Singapore's "Mile Zero," the literal center of Singapore, from which all distances were traditionally measured and all addresses took their bearings.

THE EARLY FOUNDERS' STONE

The stone became the monument itself

Outside the Fullerton Hotel by the Singapore River
MRT: Raffles Place

In an obscure corner by the Singapore River, in the shadows of the Fullerton Hotel, the Early Founders' Stone is a plain and undistinguished memorial to the nameless immigrants whose daring and endeavor laid the foundation for modern Singapore.

A block of gray granite, material with which the edifices at the beginnings of modern Singapore were raised, it rests in an almost clumsy manner on a pedestal of red bricks. Just 1½ by 1½ feet across and about a foot in height, the memorial also seems modest in size, especially in surroundings that are dominated by monuments of a much grander scale. Closer inspection of the block will reveal why this is so.

Words carved on each of the stone's four faces provide an explanation. Written in Singapore's four official languages, the words disclose that the stone is not what it seems, but in fact was to have been a forerunner of the memorial it now disguises itself as. In English, the words read:

THE FOUNDATION STONE OF THE MONUMENT IN TRIBUTE TO THE EARLY FOUNDERS OF SINGAPORE WAS LAID BY THE PRESIDENT OF THE REPUBLIC OF SINGAPORE ON THE 18TH DAY OF JANUARY 1970.

The idea for the monument was put forward by the Alumni International Singapore, a collection of associations representing alumni of the institutions of 11 countries, who had hoped to raise some $200,000 to have it built. The laying of the foundation coincided with the period during which the 150th anniversary of modern Singapore's founding was being commemorated, and to underline the intended monument's significance.

Singapore's first President, Yusof Ishak, was invited to lay the stone. A temporary site by the waterfront at Fullerton Road, a site that is very much associated with the arrival of immigrants, was selected. Despite the best efforts, insufficient funds were raised. This, plus the fact that a suitable design had not been conceived, contributed to the plans for the monument being abandoned in 1985 and the stone, intended as its foundation, became the monument itself. The stone has since made two moves. The first was in 1994, when it was uprooted for the construction of the Esplanade Bridge and moved to a temporary site in the National Archives at Canning Rise. It was returned to the area in 2010 and placed just across the road from where it originally stood.

THE PLAQUE OF ANDERSON BRIDGE

③

A piece of Egypt on Anderson Bridge

Fullerton Road

Facing the Victoria Theatre and Victoria Memorial Hall, between the twin roads along Anderson Bridge – one for pedestrians, the other for vehicles – stands a plaque that details the erection and construction of the bridge in 1909 and lists the names of those involved in the construction. The text continues with "This stone from Assouan, Egypt, was presented by Sir John Aird, Bart, on behalf of the Westminster Construction Co. Ltd."

Sir John Aird (through Westminster Construction Co. Ltd.), who was the contractor involved in putting up the abutments for the bridge, was indeed also the main contractor of the Aswan Dam in Egypt, constructed between 1899 and 1902 (now known as the Aswan Low Dam or Old Aswan Dam).

Anderson Bridge was constructed to supplement the capacity of Cavenagh Bridge, a shorter bridge standing parallel to Anderson just a minute's walk away. Cavenagh Bridge, constructed in 1869, is the oldest surviving bridge in Singapore and by the late 1880s it had become overloaded with vehicular traffic (including rickshaws and ox carts).

The bridge was opened in 1910 and was named for Sir John Anderson, Governor of the Straits Settlements and High Commissioner of the Federated Malay States. During his tenure, he helped to build up Singapore's port industry, regulate Singapore's currency system, and improve sanitation by pushing for the creation of public back lanes in the city.

Another prominent figure involved in the construction of the bridge was Robert Peirce, chief engineer to the municipalities of Penang and Singapore. He contributed to Singapore's infrastructure in the construction of reservoirs and tunnel works, and Upper and Lower Peirce Reservoirs in the central area of Singapore are named after him.

Grisly finds under Anderson Bridge

Anderson Bridge has been associated with some grisly finds, including bodies floating along the river under it. A particularly mysterious one was uncovered in the 1980s during a maintenance check, when human skeletal remains were found in a shaft between the steel girders at the end of the bridge closer to the Fullerton Hotel. Identification documents and personal belongings were found beside the skeleton, and pathologists said that the remains belonged to a man who had died between 20 to 25 years ago. His death (and how he ended up in the shaft) remains a mystery.

TAN KIM SENG FOUNTAIN

*Erected in shame and embarrassment
to commemorate Tan Kim Seng's contributions
to the first public waterworks in Singapore*

Corner of Esplanade Park opposite the Singapore Recreation Club
MRT: City Hall

Though parked in the middle of nowhere on a grassy patch along Connaught Drive steps from the Padang, the Victorian-era Tan Kim Seng Fountain, adorned with Greek Muses and Cherubs, is a beauty.

It's hard to imagine that it was erected in shame and embarrassment. This fountain commemorates Tan Kim Seng (1805–1864), the trader, property tycoon and philanthropist. Tan was born in Malacca and was educated in English, Dutch and Chinese. In the 1820s, he came to Singapore with a bit of capital to establish Kim Seng & Company. Over the next two decades, he accumulated a huge fortune and became the well-respected spokesman for Chinese affairs. He was appointed a Justice of the Peace in 1850 and in 1857 became the first Asian member of the Municipal Commission.

In 1857, after a severe drought, Tan decided to donate a sum of SG$13,000 towards building a reservoir to supply drinking water to the inhabitants of Singapore. Unfortunately, little was done with Tan's largesse and later on, the Colonial Engineer squandered the money by trying to make water flow uphill through pipes. The reservoir – now known as MacRitchie Reservoir – was finally completed in 1868, but the pumps and distribution network of pipes were not completed till 1877. By this time, Tan had long been deceased, having died in Malacca in 1864. In May 1880, the Municipal Commissioners, acting largely out of embarrassment and partly out of gratitude, made an offer to Tan Kim Seng's son, Tan Beng Swee, to erect a fountain to honour Tan's generous munificence.

With the help of William Henry Read, an old Singapore resident and Legislative Councillor living in retirement in London, the foundry of Andrew Handyside & Co was engaged to build the fountain. On 19 May 1882, the fountain was installed in Fullerton Square where it remained till 1929 when it was moved to its current location, a spot obscured by trees and idling tourist buses that sees few passersby. In 1935, there was a proposal to move the fountain "to a more imposing site" opposite Clifford Pier, but nothing came of it. In 1994, it underwent an extensive SG$1.12 million restoration, and on 28 December 2010, it was gazetted a National Monument.

REMAINS OF STAMFORD BRIDGE

The only remnants of any of the bridges along Stamford Canal

War Memorial Park
Near Esplanade Drive

At the War Memorial Park, near the entrance to the underpass to Esplanade Park, stand two small stone structures, each just about one meter high. Those lonely stone wall fragments, across the footpath from one another, each bear metal plates. One reads "1956 Stamford Bridge" and the other shows the Municipal Coat of Arms issued to Singapore, with the words "Majulah Singapura" ("Onward, Singapore," now the title of Singapore's national anthem), inscribed below the shield. On the coat of arms, the two anchors and wings represent Singapore's roles as seaport (from 1819) and air hub (since the 1937 opening of Kallang Airport, which was described by Amelia Earhart as the "aviation miracle of the East"). This coat of arms is similar to the one that can be found at Mount Emily Park.

Those two stone structures are the only remains of Stamford Bridge, which was constructed in 1956 over the Stamford Canal.

Once a freshwater stream, Stamford Canal flowed alongside Stamford Road, which was named after Sir Thomas Stamford Raffles. The road also was known as *lau chui khe* ("flowing water road" in Hokkien), as the canal would overflow and cover Stamford Road at high tide.

Stamford Bridge was one of several bridges built across the Stamford Canal. Others included Polglase Bridge (named after John Polglase, Municipal Secretary), Institution Bridge (named after Raffles Institution, which was where Raffles City is today) and Malcolm Bridge (named after Major-General Sir Neil Malcolm, General Officer Commanding Troops in Malaya).

Stamford Canal has been expanded over the years and, from the 1980s, it has been covered over and now lies underground, beneath development along Stamford Road.

All the bridges across the Canal have since been demolished except these two small structures that are the only remnants of any of the bridges along Stamford Canal.

THE FOOT OF THE SIR STAMFORD RAFFLES STATUE ⑥

Raffles with one foot planted in Malaya

Empress Place
MRT: Raffles Place

In front of the Victoria Theatre and Concert Hall (formerly the Victoria Memorial Hall) in Empress Place on the left bank of the Singapore River, the site of some of Singapore's earliest settlements, a statue erected to the memory of Sir Stamford Raffles, the founder of modern Singapore, occupies a prominent position.

From an elevated spot atop a high pedestal, Raffles, with arms folded, appears to take in the awe-inspiring sight of the modern skyscraper-dominated metropolis his trading post has become. While many of the details on the blackened bronze statue are quite visible, one rather significant detail is not: Raffles was sculpted with one foot planted on Malaya through a tracing of a map of the territory at its base, to symbolize Raffles having set foot on British Malaya.

The eight-foot statue was the work of English sculptor and poet Thomas Woolner, one of seven founding members of the Pre-Raphaelite Brotherhood. It was originally standing at the center of the Padang – a large playing field then by the sea – where it was unveiled on the occasion of the Golden Jubilee of Queen Victoria's reign on June 27, 1887.

Its undignified position – where it was all too often used as a vantage point by spectators and also subject to frequent hits by soccer balls – prompted the move to its present spot, where the British legacy in Singapore is most visible in the form of memorials and civic buildings. The move, made in February, 1919 for the centenary of Singapore's founding, also saw a semi-circular colonnade built around the rear of the statue, a marble fountain in front of it, and a commemorative tablet, as well as a bronze shield engraved with Raffles' Arms and the Knight's motto, placed on the pedestal.

The Japanese Occupation would see Raffles momentarily lose his perch. The statue was moved by the Japanese and stored in the Raffles Museum (the National Museum of Singapore today). It would be restored during the British reoccupation of Singapore in 1946, by which time the colonnade had disappeared. A polymarble replica of the statue was made on the occasion of the 150th anniversary of Singapore's founding from a mold made from Woolner's statue. The white replica stands, close to the original by the river, at what is thought to be the site where Raffles first landed.

TUDOR ROSE

*The stone had once been part of the Palace
of Westminster*

*Old Parliament House/Arts House, Level 2
MRT: City Hall*

FROM THE FABRIC OF THE
VICTORIA TOWER OF THE
PALACE OF WESTMINSTER
PRESENTED BY
HER MAJESTY'S GOVERNMENT
TO
THE SINGAPORE GOVERNMENT
15 DECEMBER 1955

High above the staircase leading to the third level of the Old Parliament House, embedded into the wall of the oldest building in Singapore is an ancient sandstone carving of a Tudor Rose. Measuring approximately 45 cm (18 inches) square, 40 cm (15 inches) deep and weighing some 114 kg (250 lbs), this modest and worn-out looking stone was once a part of the Palace of Westminster in London. On 15 December 1955, during the visit of Singapore Chief Minister David Marshall to London to discuss Singapore's constitutional future, Sir Alan Lennox-Boyd, then Secretary of State for the Colonies, presented the Tudor Rose to Marshall at a gathering comprising the Chairman and Secretary of the Commonwealth Parliamentary Association.

The stone had once been part of the Palace of Westminster and had been salvaged from the damage of the Victoria Tower when it was bombed during a German air-raid in May 1941. At the presentation, Lennox-Boyd stated that the stone would be "a political symbol of the close and affectionate understanding between the British and Singapore people." To this, Marshall replied, "We hope it will symbolise the new relationship of brotherhood and co-operation in democracy for which we are striving today and which we hope will be a reality tomorrow."

The Rose was shipped to Singapore on board the Benvenue, which arrived on 5 February 1956, but it could not be unloaded because of torrential rain. After it was unloaded the following day and unpacked, it was stored in the Public Works Department warehouse in preparation for the formal presentation ceremony to be organised by the Commonwealth Parliamentary Association in which Marshall would present it to Speaker of the Legislative Assembly, Sir George Oehlers.

This ceremony, which would permanently incorporate the Rose into the fabric of the Assembly House, did not take place and, as late as August 1956, the Rose was still in the stores of the Public Works Department. It was eventually installed in the wall on the landing of the staircase leading to the Strangers' Gallery – as proposed by the Commonwealth Parliamentary Association – where it remains. In 1999, when Parliament moved to its new building, the plan to remove the Tudor Rose and reinstall it in its new premises was abandoned for fear of damaging the Rose.

BRONZE THAI ELEPHANT

A gift from a Siamese king

1 Old Parliament Lane
MRT: City Hall

When King Chulalongkorn of Siam (1853–1910) arrived in Singapore on March 15, 1871, he became the first Siamese monarch to visit a foreign country. To commemorate the occasion, he presented Singapore with the small bronze elephant statue that today stands atop a high pedestal in front of the Old Parliament House. In Thai culture, the elephant is a revered symbol of strength and power, and Chulalongkorn's gift marked the start of a close relationship between the two countries that has endured ever since.

Originally in front of the old Town Hall (now Victoria Theatre), in a fit of statue shuffling, the elephant was moved to its current location in 1919 to make way for Woolner's bronze statue of Raffles, which was moved from the middle of Padang to its current spot in Empress Place.

Anna and the King of Siam

Chulalongkorn's father, King Mongkut (1804–1868), was a scholarly man who wanted his 82 children and 39 wives to receive a modern Western secular education. He needed a tutor who would not try to make Christians out of his family and turned to Tan Kim Ching, Siamese Consul in Singapore, for a recommendation. It was Tan who recommended teacher Anna Leonowens (1831–1915) to the King. Born near Mumbai (India) to an Anglo-Indian family (her maternal grandmother was Indian), Leonowens married her Irish-born childhood sweetheart and immigrated to Australia. When her husband died suddenly in 1859, she headed to Singapore with their two young children. To support herself and her children in the hardscrabble days of the mid-19th century, Leonowens reinvented herself by concealing her Eurasian heritage to improve her prospects. Educated, well-traveled and good with languages, she took up teaching, and before she knew it was moving to Bangkok to tutor Mongkut's brood, including the crown Prince Chulalongkorn. Leonowens spent five years as a member of the Siamese court. Her memoirs afterward formed a chain reaction of royal proportions, becoming the basis of Margaret Landon's 1944 book *Anna and the King of Siam* and Rodgers and Hammerstein's 1951 Broadway hit *The King and I*. Some historians credit Chulalongkorn's far-reaching political reforms and modern thinking to Leonowens's progressive teachings – a claim hotly disputed by the Thais.

CITY HALL CHAMBER

Hall of high jinks and high drama

National Gallery Singapore
1 St. Andrew's Road
Building Highlights Tour, daily at 11am and 3pm
MRT: City Hall

Nestled in the heart of the National Gallery Singapore and hidden from public view is a lovely two-story hall known as the City Hall Chamber.

When the building opened in April 1929, the Straits Times described the Chamber to be of "noble proportions" with polished teak panelling and "massive columns 25 feet high in Siena marble mounted on bronze bases and surmounted by bronze caps" and lit by "two great chandeliers." Today, it stills looks like that and is used as a function room within the National Gallery.

Constructed between 1925 and 1929, the City Hall building (which later, when combined with the former 1939-built Supreme Court next door, became the National Gallery) was initially the home of the Municipal Commission and was known simply as the Municipal Building. The Chamber was a boardroom. When Singapore attained "city" status in 1951, the building was renamed City Hall and remained Singapore's main government building till 1988, when it was given over to the Supreme Court for additional courtrooms. The Supreme Court occupied this building until 2006 when it moved to its own new building. Work on the restoration of the old Supreme Court Building and City Hall commenced in 2011. In 2015 it reopened as the National Gallery of Singapore.

Over the years, the Chamber was the site of many key historical events in Singapore history. In the late 1950s, it was the site of tumultuous debates of the City Council chaired by Mayor Ong Eng Guan, and on June 5, 1959, Singapore's first self-governing cabinet, led by Prime Minister Lee Kuan Yew, took their Oaths of Allegiance and Office in the Chamber. On Dec. 4, 1959, the inauguration of Singapore's head of state, Yusof Ishak, took place in the Chamber as well. The building was gazetted as a National Monument on Feb. 14, 1992.

Where the surrender of the Japanese forces took place on Sept. 12, 1945

Many older Singaporeans know the room as the "Surrender Chamber," where the surrender of the Japanese forces took place on Sept. 12, 1945, signaling the end of more than three-and-a-half years of brutal occupation. Coming full circle, in 2015, it was the venue for the commemoration of the 70th anniversary of Japan's capitulation.

LIONS ON THE ELGIN BRIDGE

*Little known sculptures of Cavaliere
Rodolfo Nolli*

*Elgin Bridge
Singapore River
MRT: Raffles Place*

The Elgin Bridge is perhaps the most important of Singapore's bridges, connecting two sections of a long-established thoroughfare that has carried traffic between the Civic District and settlements on the river's north and the main Chinese settlement in the south. The three arches of its superstructure give the bridge a rather distinctive appearance and it's on the superstructure that some of the more obscure works of the prolific Italian sculptor Cavaliere Rodolfo Nolli can be found.

The works are a set of four bronze roundels and six ornate brass lamps. The roundels, hinged along one edge, act as doors to the lamp's switch boxes. They also feature a relief in which a lion and a palm tree – the crest of the one-time Singapore Municipal Commission – are depicted, along with a rare signature of Nolli.

From the country's founding, a series of important bridges was built across the lower reaches of the Singapore River, a waterway along which much of Singapore's early wealth was built. Completed in 1929, the Elgin Bridge replaced a bridge of the same name and occupies the site of the river's first bridge: a wooden footbridge constructed in 1819. A succession of bridges replaced the footbridge as traffic increased. The first Elgin Bridge was erected in 1862 and was named after Lord Elgin, the 8th Earl of Elgin and the then-Viceroy of India.

Cavaliere Rodolfo Nolli

Hailing from an italian family of sculptors and stonemasons, Cavaliere Rodolfo Nolli came to Singapore in 1921 after an eight-year stint in Bangkok. In Bangkok, Nolli worked with an uncle on several Royal-commissioned projects. He also spent two years there as an art lecturer.

Nolli was knighted by the Italian Crown in 1925 (hence the title Cavaliere or Cav.) for his contributions overseas. He would spend much of the 35 years until his retirement in 1956 working in Singapore and also in Malaya and Brunei.

The works that brought Nolli the greatest pride were the sculptures that grace the tympanum of the majestic 1939-built Supreme Court, now part of the National Gallery Singapore. The huge sculptures, which weigh about four tons in total, depict the allegory of justice with Lady Justice, untypically, without a blindfold. These were part of a series of precast exterior decorative works that also included the granite-like granolithic cladding and the grand Corinthian columns.

PHANTOM POOL

Pool of the past

Remains of the River Valley Swimming Complex
The Foothills
70 River Valley Road
MRT: Clarke Quay

I t looks like a soccer pitch, but the flat rectangular grassy patch at the foot of Fort Canning Hill along River Valley Road, known as The Foothills, was once the location of an Olympic-size pool. One of Singapore's oldest public swimming pools, it was built in 1959 on the site of the King George V Park by the Singapore City Council and designed by British architect M. E. Crocker who also designed the Farrer Park Swimming Complex. You can still see the original entrance gates, exit turnstile, mosaic floor tiles and bathroom signage. The former changing rooms behind it survive as an events and arts space.

In its early years, the River Valley Swimming Complex drew crowds on hot Singapore afternoons. In part because of its wooded surroundings, it was also a popular hangout for gay men. However, like other mid-20th-century pools in Singapore, by the 1970s its popularity was waning. Swimming facilities were being built in the new satellite towns popping up all over the country and more people were also moving into condos with their own pools, so attendance at the once-jam-packed public ones began to dry up. As a result, many pools were abandoned and eventually closed, filled in and repurposed as parking lots, dog runs and playgrounds.

Mount Emily swimming complex: Singapore's oldest public pool

The Mount Emily Swimming Complex was Singapore's first public pool, opened in 1931 on Upper Wilkie Road. The 50-meter-long, Olympic-size fresh-water pool was converted from an old municipal reservoir built in the 1870s that provided fresh water to downtown Singapore as well as the nearby Kandang Kerbau (KK) Hospital. It could accommodate as many as 300 swimmers in one day, from the coolie class to competitive swimmers, each paying an admission fee of 10 to 20 cents. Following WWII, the British Military Administration requisitioned the pool and filled it with seawater for use by service personnel. It was handed back to the Municipality, renovated and eventually opened to the general public again, but declining use led to its eventual closure and demolition in 1981. Today, you can find a large flat rectangular park on Mount Emily, a footprint of Singapore's beloved first pool for the people.

Yan Kit Swimming Complex on Yan Kit Road in Tanjong Pagar opened in 1952 as Singapore's second public pool. Built in a densely populated part of the country, it too thrived for several decades, but by 2001 it was abandoned like many others and demolished in 2012, though the Art Deco-style changing rooms remain (to the right).

FORT CANNING LIGHTHOUSE

The first lighthouse on Singapore Island

Raffles Terrace, Fort Canning
MRT: Dhoby Ghaut

On the southern corner of Fort Canning Hill, in a plaza known as Raffles Terrace, just below "Raffles House" (a reproduction of the house Stamford Raffles had lived in two centuries ago supposedly on that site) and adjacent to a historic flagstaff and time ball, is an odd-looking "lighthouse." This is a replica of the original lighthouse that stood at the same spot from 1902 to 1958 as the first lighthouse on Singapore Island.

When the British arrived in 1819, the dense vegetation on top of Fort Canning – then known as Bukit Larangan or Forbidden Hill – was cleared and a large flagstaff erected on the site of the present flagstaff. The first one was used to not only symbolise British occupation of the island, but also as a signalling device for ships in the harbour. From about 1855, workers would climb it and hang a lantern on the top of the flagstaff. Made of timber, it had to be replaced several times because it tended to rot in the damp tropical weather, making it exceedingly dangerous for workers to clamber to the top. Towards the end of the 19th century, it was decided that a proper lighthouse should be built on Fort Canning.

The original Fort Canning Lighthouse, built by the firm of Riley, Hargreaves & Co, opened on 27 February 1902. Designed as a conical tower on semi-skeletal steel pylons, the lighthouse was 24.3 m (80 ft) tall and its lantern was powered by a vaporised kerosene burner that generated 20,000 candelas with a single white flash every 17 seconds; it could be seen 19 nautical miles (35.2 km) away. A lone light-keeper manned it.

With the waterfront area gradually populated by tall buildings, the lighthouse became increasingly obscure. In 1958, it was decided that a new lighthouse would be installed on top of the Fullerton Building, located right on the shoreline (see page 188). The Fort Canning Lighthouse shone for the last time on the night of 12 December 1958 and was later dismantled.

In 2003, a small replica of the original was built in its place. This is the only lighthouse to have been dismantled and then in a sense resurrected – though just a shadow of its dazzling predecessor.

View of Fort Canning Hill from the Singapore River (1902-3). Notice the Time Ball, the Flagstaff and the Lighthouse in the background.

FREEMASONS HALL

Yes, occasional visits are possible

23A Coleman Street
Accessible on organized tours, for instance with Jane's Singapore Tours
MRT: City Hall

Contrary to common belief, Singapore's Freemasons headquarters, in the stately Masonic Hall on Coleman Street, are open to the public occasionally through organized tours with local companies. Small groups are first told about the symbols on the outside of the building. Since freemasonry evolved from the medieval guilds of stonemasons and cathedral builders, you'll see representations of their tools, the square and compass, on the exterior. Inside, tour groups are led into the main hall where meetings are held, as well as into a small museum.

In Singapore, the oldest Freemasons Lodge was established in 1845. Its first members were lawyer and newspaper editor William Napier and businessman William H. Read. Early meetings were convened in various premises prior to the construction of the Masonic Hall on Coleman Street.

In 1879, the Freema-
sons constructed a one-
story lodge, adding a
second story later in
1888. It was built in
the English Renaissance
style, which was de
rigueur for English go-
vernment buildings in
the day. Over time the
building was mildly
altered, mainly the
removal of a porch, but
otherwise remains true
to its original aesthetic.
Inside, in addition to
the dining room, the
building houses a library
and offices, a bar, a
series of private meeting
rooms and a place called
the "temple."

There are more than
a dozen Masonic lodges
active in Singapore.

SARKIES PHANTOM TOMBS

The tombstones were moved from Bukit Timah in the early 1970s

St Gregory's Armenian Church Graveyard
60 Hill Street
MRT: City Hall

The honor of Singapore's first Christian church goes to the Armenian Apostolic Church of St. Gregory the Illuminator, known locally as the Armenian Church. It is a diminutive chapel whose size and simplicity of form endow it with a sense of humble grace and serenity. On the church grounds in a peaceful Memorial Garden, flowering trees shade carved white marble gravestones that mark the final resting place of a few prominent figures from the local Armenian community who are buried here. Or are they?

The monuments in the Memorial Garden bear the names Moses, Joaquim and Sarkies, among other well-known names to Singaporeans. It was Catchick Moses who, in 1845, established the Straits Times, which grew to become Singapore's national newspaper. Agnes Joaquim hybridized an orchid in the 1880s that is named for her, the Vanda Miss Joaquim, and would eventually be declared the national flower. And in 1887, Tigran Sarkies and his brother, Martin, opened Raffles Hotel, which is without doubt the city's most celebrated hotel.

However, none of them is actually buried here. The tombstones came from Bukit Timah Cemetery and were moved to the grounds of the Armenian Church in the early 1970s. And contrary to some reports, the Sarkies named on the stones are not any of the famous Sarkies Brothers hoteliers (there were four of them), but are likely their descendants or even from another Sarkies line altogether (there were at least two unrelated Sarkies families who settled in Singapore in the 1820s).

Singapore's Armenian community was small in numbers; fewer than 700 Armenians have lived here total. However, their impact was large, as this charming church suggests. It was built entirely by funds from the tiny but well-to-do community. Consecrated in 1836, it was designed by Irish architect George D. Coleman in a neo-classical architectural style that was popular in tropical colonial architecture. Features typical of Armenian Church architecture include the vaulted ceiling and cupola inside.

MEMORIAL TO JAMES BROOKE NAPIER

An infant mourned in grandeur

Fort Canning Park Lawn
MRT: City Hall

On top of a sloping hill in Fort Canning Park, near an old stone wall that once enclosed a cemetery, a curious whitewashed Gothic Revival structure (a design that was popular in the early 19th century) is a forgotten memorial to the infant James Brooke Napier. Just behind it is the proud, almost paternal-looking Fort Canning Centre, built in 1926 as British army barracks.

One of Singapore's first Christian cemeteries was located on Fort Canning Hill. In two burial sites, the first used from 1819 to 1822 and the second from 1822 to 1865, a large number of the port's earliest European inhabitants, now historically significant figures, and their loved ones were laid to rest.

Fort Canning was closed to burials in 1865 and eventually became a park. Graves were exhumed and, in the 1950s, their tombstones were embedded in the park walls. Most visitors today scan the wall looking for famous Colonial-era names they may recognize, but a closer look at the dates reveals a large number of children buried here, none remembered as elegantly as young James Brooke Napier.

James Brooke Napier was just five months old when he died at sea on February 17, 1848. His father, William Napier, was a prominent lawyer who founded the Singapore Free Press and also served as Lieutenant-Governor of Labuan, in Borneo, under James Brooke, the first of the White Rajahs of Sarawak, for whom the child was named. The infant's mother, Maria Frances Napier, was the widow of renowned architect George Coleman; she had married Napier just four years before James Brooke Napier was born. Coleman is responsible for much of the notable Colonial-era architecture that still exists in Singapore today.

Incidentally, George Coleman was also laid to rest in this cemetery. It is believed that the two graceful cupolas that sit downhill from the Napier memorial were designed by him. Nearby, the cemetery's two Gothic-style gates, designed by Charles Edward Faber, superintending engineer of the Straits Settlement, date back to the mid-19th century.

FORT CANNING'S TOMBSTONE WALL

The brick wall that became a curious collage of grave markers

Fort Canning
Open 24 hours
Free
MRT: Dhoby Ghaut

A top today's Fort Canning, Bishop Daniel Wilson of Calcutta consecrated the Government Hill Cemetery in 1845, and afterwards a brick wall was built around it. Today the cemetery is a grassy lawn and that wall is still there, though if you go in for a closer look you'll see it's embedded with dozens of tombstones. Those grave markers once dotted the hillside when Government Hill Cemetery was

overflowing with inhabitants. When it was eventually closed to new burials in the 1860s, it fell into disrepair and, by the 1940s, many of the tombstones had crumbled. Though no one seems to know who began the practice and when exactly it was done, by the 1950s, most of the pieces had been picked up and embedded into the wall in a most curious collage of grave markers. The inhabitants of the cemetery were exhumed in 1974 and the area renamed "The Central Park," and then re-renamed "Fort Canning Green" as it's known today. It's now a popular venue for outdoor plays and events. Few notice the two sloping sections of the wall that remains to this day.

Forbidden Hill

The original name of Fort Canning was Bukit Larangan ('Forbidden Hill'). It was one of the most sacred sites in early Singapore because the Malays believed it to be the site of a palace and ancient burial ground of royalty. Archaeological excavations in the late 1980s revealed that no burials had in fact taken place on Fort Canning before the 19th century. When the British arrived in Singapore in 1819, the hill – which was renamed Government Hill – was cleared of vegetation and, before long, some Europeans began burying their dead there. This was the first European cemetery atop Fort Canning, but it was soon relocated as it was too close to the Government Bungalow that architect G.D. Coleman built for Lieutenant-Governor Sir Stamford Raffles. A new cemetery was laid out further north on the same slope and this became the site of the aforementioned cemetery that was eventually extended all the way down the hill and contained within a brick wall. Around this time, Captain Charles Faber, superintending engineer of the Straits Settlements, built the two Gothic archways that still stand nearby, a dramatic entrance to a phantom burial ground.

Gravestone of the first person born in Colonial Singapore

The first child born in Singapore after the British arrived was Agnes Maria Bernard, born on July 25, 1819. She was the daughter of Esther Farquhar and Francis J Bernard. Esther Farquhar was the eldest daughter of Singapore's first resident, William Farquhar, while her husband, Francis Bernard, was Singapore's first "police chief." The gravestone of Agnes Maria Bernard, who died in 1854, can be seen embedded in the wall of Fort Canning.

THE MACE OF SINGAPORE

Forgotten Symbol of the City

Singapore History Gallery
National Museum, 93 Stamford Road
Daily 10am–7pm
Free for citizens and permanent residents; for visitors it's $15 for adults and $10
for seniors and students
MRT: Bras Basah or Dhoby Ghaut

Standing erect in a glass case tucked inside the Singapore History Gallery of the National Museum is Singapore's oldest and most exquisite official Mace – that of the City of Singapore. The magnificent SGD$15,000 gold Mace – the traditional symbol of authority – was commissioned to Hamilton & Inches of Edinburgh by the prominent philanthropist Loke Wan Tho to commemorate the elevation of Singapore to City status in 1951. Charles d'Orville Pilkington Jackson (1887–1973), a well-known Scottish sculptor, was invited to execute the design. It was placed on exhibition first in Edinburgh and then in London before being shipped out to Singapore in March 1954.

The Mace is rich in symbolism and its design was the outcome of many suggestions and ideas by a committee consisting of university professors, the Raffles Museum staff and Loke himself. Measuring 1.2 meters (nearly 4 feet) long, the gold Mace is embellished with heraldic symbols incorporating the coats-of-arms of Singapore, the Straits Settlements and Sir Stamford Raffles. It also bears European, Chinese, Malay and Indian figures and representations of Malayan flowers and animals. Loke presented the Mace to the President of the City Council, TPF McNeice, at a brief ceremony at the City Hall Chamber at 2:15pm on March 31, 1954. When presenting the Mace, Loke stated: "This mace is a signpost in our recorded history, pointing I hope, to a greater and nobler Singapore."

Hidden in a small, secret compartment in the Mace is a scroll giving a brief history of the colony, beginning with its establishment as a British trading post in 1819.

On Dec. 24, 1957, shortly after being elected Mayor of the City of Singapore, Ong Eng Guan ordered the Mace to be removed from the Council Chamber as it was "a relic of colonialism" and wanted it to be discarded. Ong's move was controversial and provoked heated reactions and prompted British Member of Parliament Sir John Barlow to offer to buy the Mace. The Mace never made it back into the City Council Chamber as the Council was disbanded in 1959. For many years, the Mace remained in the Boardroom of the Public Utilities Board before being transferred to the museum.

A PAUL REVERE BELL

Ringing in the Night

Singapore History Gallery
National Museum, 93 Stamford Road
Daily 10am–7pm
Free for citizens and permanent residents; for visitors it's $15 for adults and $10
for seniors and students
MRT: Bras Basah or Dhoby Ghaut

Nineteenth-century Singapore was a dangerous place after nightfall, with robberies and assaults commonplace on poorly lit streets, not to mention the very real threat of attacks by prowling tigers and panthers. Curfews were part of the fabric of life in those days, with a nightly gun fired at 8pm to remind sailors to hightail it back to their ships and to warn residents to be watchful of their surroundings. Starting in 1843, a bell made by Paul Revere was also rung.

In that year, Maria Revere Balestier (1785-1847), daughter of American patriot and bell-foundry owner Paul Revere (1735-1818) and the wife of Joseph Balestier (1788-1858), the first American Consul to Singapore, gave a Revere Bell to Singapore's Church of St. Andrew (the predecessor of St. Andrew's Cathedral). The gift came with strings attached; she required that the church ring the bell for five minutes immediately after the 8pm gunshot to make sure everyone knew curfew hours were starting.

The bell was rung at the Church of St. Andrew, and then at the new St. Andrew's Cathedral that replaced it, until 1874 when the curfew alert was discontinued. The Revere Bell was used at the church for other purposes until 1889, when it was removed and intermittently put in storage and loaned out to various parties. In 2006, it became part of the permanent exhibition of the Singapore History Gallery at the National Museum of Singapore. The Singapore bell is the only Revere Bell outside the United States.

The bell was cast in the Revere foundry in Boston, which operated between 1792 and 1828, with legendary Paul Revere himself active in the business until 1811 when he retired. An inscription on the bell reads: "Revere, Boston 1843. Presented to St Andrew's Church, Singapore, by Mrs Maria Revere Balestier of Boston, United States of America."

Paul Revere: famous for more than bells

Aside from his work as a silversmith, industrialist and bell maker, Revere was a passionate political activist and one of America's best known and, well, most revered, folk heroes. He's best known for his midnight horse ride through the Massachusetts countryside on April 18, 1775, to warn American officials and troops that the British were coming. He was responsible for the hanging of two lanterns in the bell-tower of Christ Church in Boston indicating that the British troops would be approaching "by sea" via crossing the Charles River rather than "by land."

THE SINGAPORE STONE

The mystery of the text of the Singapore Stone

Singapore History Gallery
National Museum, 93 Stamford Road
Daily 10am–7pm
Free for citizens and permanent residents; for visitors it's $15 for adults and $10
for seniors and students
MRT: Bras Basah or Dhoby Ghaut

On display at the National Museum of Singapore, welcoming visitors to the Singapore History Gallery, the piece of sandstone known as the Singapore Stone, measuring about two feet across, is part of a much larger boulder that the British "discovered" at the mouth of the Singapore River, not long after they arrived in 1819. Several lines of an ancient text are carved into its face, inscriptions that for the longest time have been a source of puzzlement.

How the huge boulder, which measured 10 by 10 feet, got to its position, is anyone's guess. If speculation among the early dwellers of Singapore is to be believed, the boulder is the very same one that a 14th-century hero named Badang tossed there in an account described in the Sejarah Melayu (Malay Annals).

Compiled in the 15th or 16th centuries, the annals are the chronicles of the kings of Malacca, the first of whom fled Singapura (Malay for Singapore) as its last king. Going back to the founding of the 14th-century kingdom of Singapura, the tales are prone to exaggeration and their historical accuracy has been called into question. Nevertheless, the compilation is considered to be an important work of Malay historical literature with anecdotal accounts of local history. Badang, a man of extraordinary strength, tosses a boulder to the mouth of the river in the tale, winning a challenge made by the Raja of Kalinga in south India. The raja's strongman, so the tale goes, failed in his attempt to lift the boulder.

The stone on display was one of three similarly sized fragments that survived an 1843 effort to have the boulder blasted out for the construction of Fort Fullerton. The fragments were recovered by a British colonel, James Low, and sent to Calcutta in 1848 for analysis. Only one was to find its way back, arriving on "indefinite loan" from the Indian Museum in 1918. All attempts to locate the two missing fragments have been unsuccessful.

The stone is thought to date back to the 10th to 14th centuries, a period when Singapore was known as Temasek. Its mysterious inscriptions, part of 50 lines of text found on the boulder, were well-weathered by the time the British found the stone. The writing is thought to be in Kawi, a script that has origins in 8th-century Java, and provides evidence of the long links Singapore, and Temasek before it, had with the rest of the world.

DRINKING FOUNTAIN AT THE NATIONAL MUSEUM OF SINGAPORE

A moving fountain

National Museum
93 Stamford Road
MRT: Bras Basah or Dhoby Ghaut

Tucked away in a corner at the outdoor terrace of the National Museum is what is believed to be Singapore's first public drinking fountain, dated 1864. Compact and unassuming, this marble water fountain was donated by John Gemmill "for the use of all nations at Singapore."

The fountain's original location is not known, but early photographs show it standing in the center of Raffles Place in 1919. It was later relocated to Empress Place where it stood in front of the Victoria Memorial Hall.

The lion head was damaged by vandals during the Japanese Occupation in the 1940s, and the shattered muzzle had apparently caused the water to cease to flow. The fountain was afterwards relocated to the National Museum in 1967.

When the museum was closed for redevelopment in 2002, the fountain was brought to the Heritage Conservation Centre for full restoration works before being returned to the National Museum.

John Gemmill was a businessman who lived in Singapore in the earlier half of the 19th century. He was a storekeeper, a banker, and the first public auctioneer in Singapore. In *One Hundred Years of Singapore*, Mr Gemmill is recorded to have issued a business circular advertising for his stock of brandy, in the context that with the founding of the first Temperance Society in Singapore, sales for wine and spirits had gone down tremendously.

Other historic fountains in Singapore include the Tan Kim Seng Fountain (see page 54) and the cast-iron fountain at the Raffles Hotel.

John Gemmill and the Gemmill Lane

Gemmill Lane, a narrow street between Club Street and Amoy Street at the foot of Ann Siang Hill, was named for him. In fact, Ann Siang Hill itself used to be known as Gemmill's Hill and was where John Gemmill lived before it was sold to Chia Ann Siang. Though short in length, Gemmill Lane is today home to several stylish bars and restaurants.

OLD LIBRARY GATE PILLARS

The Gate to Nowhere

Near National Museum of Singapore
93 Stamford Road
MRT: Dhoby Ghaut

Just east of the National Museum of Singapore property and now a part of the open air courtyard area of the new Singapore Management University (SMU) building, stand a pair of red brick pillars. Just behind them is a section of old white fence. The posts seem lost and have little purpose or connection with their surroundings except perhaps to beckon visitors to pass through them and take the escalators just beyond them up to Fort Canning Hill.

In fact, at one time the pillars had marked the entrance to a building of much social significance, the National Library.

Completed in 1960, the public building with its red brick face (that the pillars matched), was one of several built in Singapore's transition from a British colony to eventual independence. It symbolized Singapore's coming of age.

Built partly through the contributions of philanthropist and rubber magnate Lee Kong Chian, it was Singapore's first purpose-built public library, though not the country's first public library. Membership was free and open to all.

Over the years the library building, though built with function rather than form in mind, had become an architectural icon and a proud symbol. It also served as an important social space, enough so that when plans to demolish the beloved building were announced in the 1990s, it unleashed an unprecedented show of displeasure from the relatively docile Singaporean public.

Despite the apparent resistance, the authorities moved ahead with the demolition. The library was moved to a new building on Victoria Street in 2004 and the old building was demolished the following year so that a road tunnel could be built to improve the area's traffic flow. While the outcome may not have been a positive one for the general public, the episode raised awareness of and interest in heritage conservation in Singapore. It is thought now to have been a catalyst to more robust community participation in the preservation of public spaces and buildings that has led to several positive outcomes in the years since.

A number of bricks from the old National Library also have been preserved in a wall in a basement garden of the new library.

THE ORGAN OF THE CATHEDRAL OF THE GOOD SHEPHERD

Singapore's Oldest Pipe Organ

Corner of Orchard Road and Queen Street
cathedral.catholic.sg
MRT: Bras Basah or City Hall

The beautifully restored 19th-century Renaissance-style Cathedral of the Good Shepherd on Queen Street at Orchard Road is not only Singapore's oldest Roman Catholic church, the pipe organ in its west gallery – or at least the original 918-pipe central section of the organ – is Singapore's oldest. The working organ now has an especially grand appearance and features an unsymmetrical 1882 pipe façade.

Pipe organs are a rare find in Singapore as their use has mainly been confined to Christian worship. The first was installed as far back as the 19th century and less than a dozen exist today, mostly hidden away in churches.

The original section of the Cathedral's organ, which was tropicalized and installed by locally-based musical instrument dealer W. J. Garcia, has a well-established pedigree. It was produced by London-based Bevington and Sons, a renowned English organ builder. The organ was a replacement for an older organ that the Cathedral had acquired from another church and was first heard at its dedication on October 20, 1912.

The organ has survived both the ravages of time and of war. Though not damaged by direct military action, the organ saw its parts scavenged for their materials during the Japanese Occupation. Kept in working order for large parts of its life through a series of restorations and refurbishments, the organ has had parts replaced and has also been modified with additions made. Restoration and repair efforts in the 1980s, undertaken by local organ builder Robert Navaratnam, added pipes salvaged from a Hill, Norman & Beard organ at the Victoria Memorial Hall that was also damaged during the Occupation.

More recently, the pipe organ was dismantled and shipped to Diego Cera Organ Builders in Las Piñas in the Philippines for a complete overhaul as part of the restoration of the Cathedral. Reinstalled in 2016, the restored organ was heard again at the Cathedral's reopening mass on November 20 of the same year.

Recitals, which are open to all, are now held on a regular basis. Further information on this can be found on the Cathedral's website.

BABY GATE OR THE GATE OF HOPE

The sorrowful story behind Chijmes

Chijmes (formerly the Convent of the Holy Infant Jesus or CHIJ)
Victoria Street
MRT: City Hall

Chijmes (pronounced "chimes") is renowned for fine dining, fun pubs and chill cafes, a rather irreverent repurposing for a restored 19th-century Roman Catholic nunnery, whose Gothic cloisters harbor a sorrowful history.

In the outer wall along Victoria Street, a small, nondescript doorway, known as "The Gate of Hope," once received countless unwanted babies left by their families. Most of those babies died.

Some only hours old, the babies were given over to the orphanage here, which was added a year after the Convent of the Holy Infant Jesus (CHIJ) was established in 1854. They came from unwed mothers, poor families and broken homes, and were predominantly female, Chinese and sickly or even dead. Some who were certain to die were sent away by families afraid that a death in the home would attract bad luck.

"The Baby Gate," as it was also known, took in unknown numbers of hapless little bundles. The Straits Times in 1946 reported that 10 years before the orphanage had received 400 babies in one year. During the Japanese Occupation, that figure jumped to 100 babies every month.

From the Straits Times report: "When the babies are taken into the Convent they are examined, washed and dressed in little white cotton shirts which have been made by the older children, and put into a cot – usually to die. These dying babies lie side by side in their cots a few yards from the stream of traffic passing down Stamford Road."

Those lucky to survive were educated at the convent school and grew to either become sisters of the order or wives to young men who called on their priests to find them a suitable match.

The orphanage closed in 1983, when the government acquired the land. The order deconsecrated the chapel and moved the convent school to Toa Payoh to make way for the CHIMJES complex that occupies the site today.

An unusual history for a place that today is associated with revelry and breaking bread. However, if the thought of wining and dining here now feels suddenly morbid, take heart that Singapore today has the world's third lowest infant mortality rate in the world.

STAINED GLASS WINDOWS AT JACOB BALLAS CENTRE

Chagall-inspired windows

24–26 Waterloo Street
Monday–Friday 9am–6pm, Sunday 9am–12:30pm, closed on Saturday
MRT: Bras Basah

In Singapore's colonial core, on the upper floors of the building facing Waterloo Street, the Jacob Ballas Centre boasts beautiful blue and gold stained glass windows. If you look carefully, you may notice how these locally-made windows resemble those made in 1962 by the famous Jewish artist Marc Chagall (1887-1985) for the Abbell Synagogue at Hadassah Ein Karem Hospital in Jerusalem.

Chagall's original windows number 12 in all, signifying Jacob's blessings on his 12 sons and Moses' blessings on the 12 tribes of Israel.

Built next to the Maghain Aboth Synagogue (1878), the older of only two synagogues in Singapore (the other is the 1905 Chesed-El Synagogue on Oxley Rise), the Jacob Ballas Centre opened in 2007.

The Centre, with function rooms, offices, kosher restaurant and accommodation for the rabbis, was a bequest of prominent Singaporean philanthropist Jacob Ballas (1921-2000), who left more than SGD$100 million to Singaporean and Israeli charities. His other big bequest was the Jacob Ballas Children's Garden, which also opened in 2007 and was carved out of the northeastern corner of the Singapore Botanic Gardens. Hedgerow mazes, wobbling rope bridges and a tree house built amidst a cluster of Banyan trees are all part of Ballas's dream park for kids. He made it clear in his will that only visitors with children in tow are allowed in, and on any day you see school groups, birthday party revelers and tots on playdates running through the water sprinklers.

From bread seller to stockbroker

Ballas was a self-made man, the only child of a poor Orthodox Jewish Baghdadi family that moved to Singapore when he was a child, at 19 Wilkie Road. His mother could barely scrape together the few cents for his school lunch money at St. Andrew's School, says classmate Jock Oehlers in his memoir *That's How It Goes: Autobiography of a Singapore Eurasian*. She made ends meet by baking matzah, the unleavened Jewish bread, which young Jacob sold around the neighborhood. Ballas made good on all of their hard work. After slogging away in car sales and insurance, he eventually became a successful stockbroker and then chairman of the Malaysian and Singapore Stock Exchange.

EX MALAYAN MOTORS SHOWROOM

㉕

A reminder of the former motoring trade on Orchard Road

14 Orchard Road
MRT: Dhoby Ghaut

With its distinctive, scallop-edged arched gable, 14 Orchard Road was meant to be noticed. But as with all old edifices found along Singapore's busy shopping mile, it has become lost in the shuffle of modern high-rise shopping malls that now dominate the street.

A mix of Art Deco and Modernist styles, the building has several interesting features. Long columns of windows carry natural light to its insides. Openings, to permit natural ventilation, blend into its façade as if they were part of the decoration. There is, of course, the arched gable, a gorgeous fan-like sweep that has been likened by some to a giant billboard. To others it resembles the Dutch Colonial-style houses ubiquitous in Amsterdam. Along with a defunct ramp that permitted vehicular access between its first and second levels, the features were well intended. A little-known fact today is that the building, currently used by a private school, was built as an auto showroom for Malayan Motors, whose portfolio of brands included Morris and Rolls-Royce.

At the time the showroom was built, auto dealers had already established themselves on Orchard Road. The first to set up shop did so within a decade of the 1896 arrival of Singapore's first automobile. A late addition to what had become known as the street's "motoring end," No. 14 was built so that it would stand out among a crowd of showrooms.

No. 14's design reflected the progressive thinking of its architect, D.S. Petrovich, who was from the prolific firm Swan & Maclaren. Its gable could only be constructed with state-of-the-art building methods such as the use of reinforced concrete, a then-recent innovation. The building endures within Orchard Road's only surviving row of street-facing pre-war houses and provides a sense of what Orchard Road looked like before the modern shopping malls arrived in the 1970s, the beginning of the end for the motoring trade on Orchard Road. Two of the street's first modern malls, The Orchard (since demolished) and Lucky Plaza (still standing) came up on sites connected to the country's early automotive industry. The former was converted from the Orchard

Motors showroom and the latter was built on the site of Champion Motors. The last of the motor traders, which included Malayan Motors, moved out in the late 1980s. This paved the way for the street to become, as some in Singapore have put it, "completely malled."

M for Manasseh Meyer

Chesed-El Synagogue
2 Oxley Rise
To visit, send a request to info@chesedel.org
MRT: Dhoby Ghaut

The Chesed-El Synagogue was designed by prolific Swan & Maclaren architect R.A.J. Bidwell, who designed many prominent buildings, including the Atbara House on Gallop Road, Eden Hall, Goodwood Park Hotel, Raffles Hotel and the Victoria Concert Hall.

As though branding his personal property, its builder Sir Manasseh Meyer (1846-1930) had the letter "M" worked into the decorative molding below the ceiling and also in the metal railings of the upper-story balcony of Chesed-El. "M" for Meyer and apparently "M" for "magnificent"–

that's how scientist Albert Einstein described Chesed-El on a visit in 1922.

Born in Bagdad, Iraq, and educated in India, Meyer emigrated to Singapore in 1861. Becoming one of Singapore's most prominent Jewish businessmen and property owners, he was knighted in 1920. He even has a street named after him in Katong. Meyer is responsible for building the country's only two synagogues, both national monuments designed with ornate plasterwork and cornices, Roman columns, arches and pilaters and, in one of them, his initials.

The Maghain Aboth synagogue was built in 1878 on Waterloo Street, originally (and ironically) called Church Street, in Singapore's then Jewish Quarter. At the time it was customary for a synagogue to be within walking distance of home. It's considered the oldest synagogue in Southeast Asia.

When Meyer had a falling out with that congregation years later, he was rich and powerful enough to leave and build his own private synagogue. In 1905, he built the Chesed-El synagogue on the grounds of his expansive estate on Oxley Rise that he called Belle Vue. The property's main house was originally built by surgeon-general Dr. Thomas Oxley in 1842 and named Killiny House. It was demolished in the 1980s to make way for a condo.

His initial "M" was also fashioned into the spindles of Eden Hall's interior wrought-iron balustrade (see page 146).

Jewish traders in Singapore

A handful of Jewish traders were in Singapore when Raffles arrived in 1819. By the outbreak of WWII, there were more than 1,500 Jewish people living in Singapore. Most were Sephardic Jews from modern-day Iraq, originally making their fortunes in the opium trade, and later rubber, tin, textiles, real estate and stocks. Today, a few thousand Jews live in Singapore, including decendents of the Sephardic Jewish Sassoon, Solomon, Benjamin and Marshall families, as well as Ashkenazi Jewish expatriates whose origins are in Eastern Europe.

SHOPHOUSE AT NO. 1 TANK ROAD ㉗

The Last Chettiar Kittangi

1 Tank Road
MRT: Clarke Quay

At first glance, the three-story shophouse at No. 1 Tank Road near the Hindu Sri Thendayuthapani Temple looks rather uninteresting. Its doors are usually closed, but if you do get a chance to peek into it, you will see that what lies hidden is a hall in which time seems to have stood still.

Long and narrow and with a low platform raised by about half a foot on either side of a passageway, the hall is laid out in the unassuming manner of the Chettiar-run money-lending establishments once found along Market Street. These offered quick and ready capital particularly to small businesses. They were very much a part of the scene in Singapore's commercial quarter since the 1820s when the Chettiars first arrived until the 1970s when the shophouses at Market Street were demolished.

Each shophouse, known as a *kittangi*, which translates into "warehouse," was really a communal working and living space and could hold as many as 50 individually-run moneylending businesses. The Chettiars, men who left their families behind in India, lived simply and had their meals supplied from the *kittangi*'s kitchen. Business was conducted from a small space each rented with transactions taking place across a low desk known as a *mejai peti*. A cotton rollaway bed, a desk and other simple items of furniture such as a cabinet holding cash, jewelery held in collateral, accounting books, notes and a few personal items was all that the Chettiars would have had in their possession.

The Chettiars hail from Chettinad, a region in India's southernmost state of Tamil Nadu and where the majority of Indian Singaporeans trace their roots. Long established as merchants and financiers, they moved across Asia and were also found in Sri Lanka, Burma and Vietnam. The loans they offered, usually subject to high interest rates, often required nothing more than a promissory note.

Events of the 20th century, the introduction of greater regulation in the financial industry and the expansion of banks and financial institutions in Singapore would see the Chettiars' business decline. From as many as 400 Chettiar moneylenders registered in the 1950s, they numbered about 50 by the 1970s when urban redevelopment would see many of the *kittangis* disappear. Today, the *kittangi* at Tank Road is the only physical reminder of the "warehouses." Business is no longer conducted here and the premises now serve as a meeting and recreational space for the Chettiars and their families who have remained in Singapore.

GATE PILLARS OF NAN CHIAU HIGH SCHOOL

A colorful past

Kim Yam Road
Close to 46 Kim Yam Road
MRT: Dhoby Ghaut or Clarke Quay

Quiet and primarily residential, Kim Yam Road isn't a typical place for a stroll. Other than a delightful row of Early Style single-story townhouses (originally warehouses, they remind of the area's mercantile past due to its proximity to the Singapore River) close to the street's intersection with Mohamed Sultan Road, there seems little of interest.

Just across from the row, however, is a curious pair of gate pillars with words in Chinese for Nan Chiau High School.

While the school's founding is connected to luminary Tan Kah Kee and the Singapore Hokkien Huay Kuan (a clan association) for which Tan served as chairman, there also are links to another successful businessman, Lee Kong Chian.

Nan Chiau High School began as an all girls' school in 1947 on premises previously used as a teachers' college that Tan and the clan association established in 1941 on land donated by Lee. The college did not quite take off due to the threat of war looming large just a year into its formation, and was instead used for a few years as the headquarters of Dalforce, a hastily formed army of Chinese volunteers that Tan helped start.

Moved to Sengkang in 2000, the school was destroyed, except for the two pillars and for one of the school's buildings that can be seen after a walk up the road past the former Tai Wah Garment Factory at 58 Kim Yam Road. Perched atop a hillock at 46 Kim Yam Road, it may, however, be quite unrecognizable in its disguise as "The Herencia," a commercial complex housing a hodgepodge of businesses.

Note, at press time, there was some construction near the pillars; we're hoping they won't be removed or destroyed.

Clan associations and schools

Founded in 1840, the Singapore Hokkien Huay Kuan is one of many Chinese clan associations. Formed along lines of kinship or place of origin, these self-help societies played an important role providing support to immigrants arriving to Singapore from China. Clan associations have also placed great emphasis on education. The Singapore Hokkien Huay Kuan, through the efforts of Tan Kah Kee (even before he became its chairman), has links to six schools including Nan Chiau. Though clan-linked schools are now run by the State, the clan associations still maintain strong ties with these schools.

CHEE GUAN CHIANG HOUSE

Forgotten beauty

25 Grange Road
MRT: Somerset

Sandwiched between towering apartment blocks and further obscured by over-grown trees lies one of Singapore's most outstanding Art Deco gems – the abandoned Chee Guan Chiang House, also known as Wellington House. Although it is surrounded by a fence, you can catch a glimpse of the house if you walk along Grange Road and peer between the Indian High Commission and the Grange Infinite condo tower.

This house, and the smaller adjacent one, were designed and built in the 1930s by Ho Kwong Yew (1903–1942), one of Singapore's earliest and leading architects of the Modern Movement. The smaller building is the older of the two and was Chee Guan Chiang's original home.

The streamlined design with its curved verandahs and cantilevered flat roofs was praised by the local press at the time as a wonderful example of the budding new Modernist aesthetic in Singapore. Ho also built the splendid six-domed Haw Par Villa (see page 178) for the Aw Brothers in 1937 that was demolished right after WWII. Sadly, at the height of his successful career, Ho was killed by the Japanese Army soon after they invaded Singapore in 1942. His three sons – Kok Hoe, Kok Kit and Kok Yin – continued his architectural practice, Ho Kwong Yew & Sons, through the 1980s.

The Chee house is named for prominent businessman Chee Guan Chiang, oldest son of the Malacca-born tycoon and philanthropist Chee Swee Cheng, who was the first chairman of the Oversea-Chinese Banking Corporation (OCBC). The elder Chee grew the family fortune in a variety of ways, owning rubber, coconut and tapioca plantations, plus interests in opium, liquor and ice. He kept mansions not only in Singapore but in Malacca as well. Chee Swee Cheng, who died just as the house was ready for occupation, is remembered by the inclusion of his initials in the design of the main gates.

In 2008, the Urban Redevelopment Authority (URA) declared the Chee mansion a conservation building. The house and its surrounding compound, which is now owned by Lee Tat Development Pte Ltd, remain in limbo thanks largely to a decades-long legal wrangle over easement rights. Given the size and the location of the land it sits on, the property is worth many millions of dollars.

THE COLONNADE

An overlooked complex stack of blocks by famed architect Paul Rudolph

82 Grange Road
MRT: Scotts Road/Orchard

Among the more humdrum high-rise apartment towers of Grange Road, it's easy to drive or walk past the peculiar-looking complex called The Colonnade without noticing its quirky geometry.

Perched atop tall cylindrical pillars of varying heights, The Colonnade comprises four quadrants that each begin and end at a different elevation. Each is composed of stacks of projecting blocks cantilevered forward of the structural columns.

Commissioned by the prominent Kwee family of the Pontiac Land Group and designed by American architect Paul Rudolph, the complex is made of reinforced concrete and covered with masonry paint.

Rudolph was known for favoring concrete and complex floor plans. In the case of The Colonnade, Rudolph's interest in modularity and interlocking spaces is clear-cut. He was fond of the architectural use of prefabricated units, which he referred to as the "twentieth-century brick." However, while The Colonnade has a prefab look, it actually wasn't built that way due to technical and financial reasons at the time.

Paul Rudolph: one of the great architects of the late-modern period

Chair of Yale University's Department of Architecture for six years, Paul Rudolph (1918-1997) is widely considered one of the great architects of the late-modern period. His most famous work is the Art and Architecture building at Yale, also known as Rudolph Hall: the chunky fortress-like building of textured concrete with a complicated floor plan is one of the earliest (1963) and most notable examples of Brutalist architecture in the United States.

By the 1970s, Paul Rudolph and his designs had fallen out of favor in the US and so he turned East. Of Rudolph's handful of post-modern Southeast Asia projects, two were built in Singapore in the 1980s – the 27-floor Colonnade, and the 45-story Concourse building on Beach Road. Both are tall, striking structures that stand apart from the crowd.

Rudolph has described the Concourse as a "whirling dervish" for its unique dynamic asymmetry of columns and stacked and interlocking clusters. It also has been called an inverted pagoda.

In Surabaya (Indonesia), Rudolph is also the architect behind the stunning Intiland Tower, another example of his obsession with cantilevered blocks.

Selegie Road, Little India and Kampong Glam

1. BUILDINGS OF MIDDLE ROAD'S EARLY COMMUNITIES   *110*
2. ELLISON BUILDING'S CUPOLAS   *114*
3. THE SUNBURST OF MASJID ABDUL GAFFOOR   *116*
4. GODDESS KALI WITH A BITE   *118*
5. NIGHT SOIL VENTS   *120*
6. ORIGINAL GATE TO "THE NEW WORLD" AMUSEMENT PARK   *122*
7. PETAIN ROAD TOWNHOUSES   *124*

⑧ JALAN KUBOR CEMETERY 126

⑨ ZUBIR SAID'S PIANO 128

⑩ THE SOY SAUCE BOTTLE BOTTOMS OF THE
SULTAN MOSQUE 130

⑪ THE LEANING MINARET OF HAJJAH FATIMAH
MOSQUE 132

⑫ GASHOLDER FRAME 134

BUILDINGS OF MIDDLE ROAD'S EARLY COMMUNITIES

The star of David on the David Elias building

270 Middle Road
MRT: Dhoby Ghaut or Bras Basah

Astroll down Middle Road, one of Singapore's oldest streets, doesn't seem particularly interesting at first glance, but upon closer inspection, traces of its colorful history reveal themselves in vestiges of the communities for whom the street had once been a home away from home.

Decorated with the Star of David, the 1928-built David Elias building near the junction with Selegie Road recalls the Mahallah, a

neighborhood of Sephardic Jews who gave the area a feel of old Baghdad. Designed by Swan & Maclaren in a style popular in the 1920s, the neo-classical building features a broad high-pitched roof, cantilevered bay windows and Italianate balconies. It housed the offices of Elias' firm, D. J. Elias and Company. Elias was the son-in-law and a relation of the prominent Joseph Aaron Elias, after whom Elias Road in Pasir Ris is named.

Laid out in Lieutenant Jackson's Town Plan of 1822, Middle Road was to have had a different destiny. A street running down the middle of the town, hence its name, it was to separate the European settlement from the civic district. The colony outgrew the plan, however, and others began to populate the area, including the Jewish community in the late 1800s and the Japanese in the early 1900s (see below).

Two more buildings are connected to the Japanese, another of the street's past communities. One cuts an unassuming figure at 250 Middle Road next to the David Elias building. Now a private school, little about it would suggest that its origins are in a Japanese hospital, the Doh-jin. The second is the Stamford Arts Centre, found just two blocks away at 155 Waterloo Street and built as a Japanese elementary school in 1920. The two span a period when Middle Road was *Chuo Dori* or Central Street, and points to there having been a sizeable Japanese community before World War II.

The pre-World War II Japanese community at Middle Road

Women in the vice trade formed the bulk of the early Japanese arrivals. The booming brothel business, centered at Malay and Hylam Streets (where Bugis Junction is today), attracted Japanese traders to nearby Middle Road to sell the "working girls" things like kimonos, flowers and drugs. Their businesses and homes would give Middle Road a distinctly Japanese flavor and it became known to the community as Chuo Dori. The war, and the eventual defeat of the Japanese and the confiscation of their property, would put a halt to the relationship.

For more information about the history and symbolism of the star of David, see the following double page spread.

The star hexagram: a magical talisman?

The hexagram – also known as the Star of David or the Shield of David – comprises two interlaced equilateral triangles, one pointing upwards and the other downwards. It symbolises the combination of man's spiritual and human nature. The six points correspond to the six directions in space (north, south, east and west, together with zenith and nadir) and also refer to the complete universal cycle of the six days of Creation (the seventh day being when the Creator rested). Hence, the hexagram became the symbol of the macrocosm (its six angles of 60° totalling 360°) and of the union between mankind and its creator. If, as laid down in the Old Testament (*Deuteronomy* 6:4–9), the hexagram (*mezuzah* in Hebrew) is often placed at the entrance to a Jewish home, it was also adopted as an amulet by Christians and Muslims. So it is far from being an exclusively Jewish symbol.

In both the Koran (38:32 et seq.) and *The Thousand and One Nights*, it is described as an indestructible talisman that affords God's blessing and offers total protection against the spirits of the natural world, the djinns. The hexagram also often appears in the windows and pediments of Christian churches, as a symbolic reference to the universal soul. In this case, that soul is represented by Christ – or, sometimes, by the pair of Christ (upright triangle) and the Virgin (inverted triangle); the result of the interlacing of the two is God the Father Almighty. The hexagram is also found in the mediated form of a lamp with six branches or a six-section rose window. Although present in the synagogue of Capernaum (3rd century AD), the hexagram does not really make its appearance in rabbinical literature until 1148 – in the *Eshkol Hakofer* written by the Karaite* scholar Judah Ben Elijah. In Chapter 242 its mystical and apotropaic (evil-averting) qualities are described, with the actual words then often being engraved on amulets: "And the names of the seven angels were written on the *mazuzah* ... The Everlasting will protect you and this symbol called the Shield of David contains, at the end of the *mezuzah*, the written name of all the angels."

In the 13th century the hexagram also became an attribute of one of the seven magic names of Metatron, the angel of the divine presence associated with the archangel Michael (head of the heavenly host and the closest to God the Father). The identification of Judaism with the Star of David began in the Middle Ages. In 1354 King Karel IV of Bohemia granted the Jewish community of Prague the privilege of putting the symbol on their banner. The Jews embroidered a gold star on a red background to form a standard that became known as the Flag of King David (*Maghen David*) and was adopted as the official symbol of Jewish synagogues. By the 19th century, the symbol had spread throughout the Jewish community. Jewish mysticism has it that the origin of the hexagram was directly linked with the flowers that adorn the menorah** – irises with six petals.

For those who believe this origin, the hexagram came directly from the hands of the God of Israel, the six-petal iris not only reassembling the Star of David in general form but also being associated with the people of Israel in the *Song of Songs*. As well as offering protection, the hexagram was believed to have magical powers. This reputation originates in the famous *Clavicula Salomonis* (Key of Solomon), a grimoire (textbook of magic) attributed to Solomon himself but, in all likelihood, produced during the Middle Ages. The anonymous texts probably came from one of the numerous Jewish schools of the Kabbalah that then existed in Europe, for the work is clearly inspired by the teachings of the Talmud and the Jewish faith. The *Clavicula* contains a collection of thirty-six pentacles (themselves symbols rich in magic and esoteric significance) which were intended to enable communication between the physical world and the different levels of the soul. There are various versions of the text, in numerous translations, and the content varies between them. However, most of the surviving texts date from the 16th and 17th centuries – although there is a Greek translation dating from the fifteenth.

In Tibet and India, the Buddhists and Hindus read this universal symbol of the hexagram in terms of the Creator and his Creation, while the Brahmins hold it to be the symbol of the god Vishnu. Originally, the two triangles were in green (upright triangle) and red (inverted triangle). Subsequently, these colours became black and white, the former representing the spirit, the latter the material world. For the Hindus, the upright triangle is associated with Shiva, Vishnu and Brahma (corresponding to the Christian God the Father, Son and Holy Ghost). The Son (Vishnu) can be seen to always occupy the middle position, being the intercessor between things divine and things earthly.

* qara'im *or* bnei mikra: *"he who follows the Scriptures". Karaism is a branch of Judaism that defends the sole authority of the Hebrew Scripture as the source of divine revelation, thus repudiating oral tradition.*

** Menorah – *the multibranched candelabra used in the rituals of Judaism. The arms of the seven-branched menorah, one of the oldest symbols of the Jewish faith, represent the seven archangels before the Throne of God: Michael, Gabriel, Samuel, Raphael, Zadkiel, Anael and Kassiel.*

- 113 -

ELLISON BUILDING'S CUPOLAS ②

Once one of the highest points in the area

Corner of Selegie and Rochor Canal roads
MRT: Little India

One of the most noticeable features of the Ellison Building is its rounded façade punctuated by a pair of rooftop cupolas and second-story balconies. But they're not just pretty flourishes. While today the Ellison Building is dwarfed by Singapore's sky-high office and apartment towers, the cupolas were once among the highest points in the area. Inside, the who's who of early 20th century Singapore would gather to view the nearby horse races on Race Course Road. Singapore's first major racecourse was located at the edge of Little India; in the 1930s it moved to Bukit Timah and then in 2000 to Kranji where it remains.

The Ellison Building was constructed in 1924 by Isaac Ellison, a Romanian Jew, for his wife Flora, a Baghdadi Jew from Rangoon. At the time, the area around Mount Sophia was popular with the local Jewish community clustered around the Maghain Aboth Synagogue on Waterloo Street.

A testament to the community, four years after the construction of the Ellison Building, the David Elias Building popped up nearby on Selegie Road, also bearing the Star of David. Both buildings have survived.

A small Star of David is visible in a pediment between the cupolas, bearing the building's name and date.

Conservation Victory

In 2008, when the Ellison Building was officially gazetted for conservation, the government recognized the social importance of the building. However, in August 2016, it was announced that three sections of the building (including the north-facing cupola) would be partly torn down to accommodate the underground construction of a new expressway and then later the affected parts would be reconstructed. This displeased local conservationists who argued that reconstruction of historical buildings is technically a falsification of historical artifacts. The government eventually compromised, figuring out a way to leave the cupola intact – a small victory for heritage conservation in Singapore.

THE SUNBURST OF MASJID ABDUL GAFFOOR

A sunburst that represents the 25 prophets mentioned in the Qur'an

41 Dunlop Street
Little India
5:30am–8:30pm
MRT: Rochor

Often overlooked by passers-by, the pretty Masjid Abdul Gaffoor mosque is wedged into a plot that is almost entirely surrounded by tall shophouses that flank narrow Dunlop Street. The mosque stands out for its Moorish and Greco-Roman motifs, including arches and Corinthian columns. What many don't notice is the interesting sundial-like starburst above the main entrance to the prayer hall. The sunburst is designed with 25 rays of light – the number 25 probably stands for the number of prophets mentioned in the Qur'an.

One could be forgiven for thinking this place is tiny, but surprisingly, it can accommodate up to 4,000 worshippers because of a creative restoration that took place in the mid 1990s, when after falling into disrepair, the mosque underwent an extensive overhaul. The entire structure was reinforced with micro-piles. Underneath, a sub-basement was deepened and enlarged to expand available prayer space. This move was a world first, creating a basement beneath an existing masonry structure while completely changing the foundation system. The restoration also lovingly repaired the architectural details and design elements, including delicate cinquefoil arched openings leading into the main prayer hall (the word cinquefoil comes from the French *cinq feuilles* meaning "five leaves.")

Kampong Kapoor

In the mid-1800s, this area, called Kampong Kapoor, bustled with industry (Indian traders, lime kilns for brickmaking, tanneries for curing leather, slaughterhouses) all employing large numbers of workers from south India. In 1859, a simple structure made of wood and tiles, named Masjid Al-Abrar, was built here for Muslim worship. In 1887, Shaik Abdul Gaffoor bin Shaik Hyder, the chief clerk in a prestigious local law firm, gained a permit for eight shophouses and nine sheds around the mosque. More shophouses were added in 1903, and the proceeds from these buildings provided the funds to build a new mosque at the site. The mosque was completed in 1910 and named after him. Abdul Gaffoor Mosque was gazetted as a national monument in 1979.

GODDESS KALI WITH A BITE

A shockingly gory statue of Kali

Sri Veeramakaliamman Temple
141 Serangoon Road
6295–4538
www.sriveeramakaliamman.com
5:30am–12:30pm and 4pm–9:30pm
MRT: Little India

Behind the main part of the Sri Verramakaliamman Temple in Little India where few wander, and shielded from the street by the high walls of the compound, lurks a gruesome figure to which devotees pay homage. Here the temple's "patron saint" Kali is portrayed, in a gold-framed niche, ripping out the insides of an evil-doer, dead and limp across her lap. Kali's eyes are crazed and her mouth bloodied and relentless. Above the niche on top of the compound's wall is another depiction showing Kali in the aftermath of having savagely killed two villains, entrails hanging down from her sharp teeth. The graphic statues deliver a crystal-clear message about what happens to bad people.

In Hinduism, Kali is the mother of the universe, embodying the duality of being a mother – loving, yet fiercely and even violently protective. One statue portrays Kali sharing a peaceful family moment with her sons Ganesha and Murugan. She appears in various forms and avatars on the inside and outside of the temple, sometimes with many sets of hands, a red face and burning hair to symbolize her omnipotence and intensity.

Sri Verramakaliamman is a National Monument with an ornate gopuram (tower), a tiered pyramid of brightly painted figures of Hindu deities and symbols, typical of the flamboyant style of south Indian Hindu temples (in contrast, temples of northern India are much more subdued). Most are warm, smiling and life-affirming portrayals of various gods and goddesses in the Hindu pantheon, unlike the Kali statue out back.

Kali has always been popular in Bengal, in eastern India, the birthplace of the laborers who built the first temple on the site in 1881, and who looked to the fierce goddess to protect them from harm. Today the Bengali laborers who toil to build Singapore's gleaming apartment and office towers still visit the temple on their day off to pay their respects and ask for blessings.

The English word "thug," as in criminal, comes from the Sanskrit word *thuggee*, meaning "concealment," which was adopted by a gang of mafia-like assassins who operated in 13th- to 19th-century India. This group's members were infamous for carrying out their ritualistic assassinations in the name of the Hindu Goddess Kali.

NIGHT SOIL VENTS

Back lane bathrooms

Backlanes of Race Course & Chander Roads
Little India
MRT: Little India

Back alleys can be fascinating places to explore in Singapore. Look down as you stroll along one that cuts behind the old buildings on Race Course and Chander roads in Little India, between Kerbau Road

and Rotan Lane, and you'll see square indentations the size of an oven door a few inches above the ground. The openings are defunct night soil doors, which you will also spot in the back lanes behind many old shophouses and buildings in Joo Chiat, Tanjong Pagar, Chinatown and Geylang.

The system started in the mid-19th century. People would go to the toilet inside a bucket or chamber pot that was positioned under a wide wooden plank or below a rudimentary seat with a hole. Early each morning, night soil collectors would go on their rounds, collecting the full buckets by opening the night soil ports in the back lanes or sometimes in separate outhouses. Dirty containers would be pulled out and covered with a lid, and replaced with clean receptacles. If there wasn't an external night soil vent, the collectors had to enter the dwellings and walk through apartments and sometimes up stairs to collect the smelly pails of waste, then lug the heavy sloshing mess back through the house to exit.

The men would carry the filled buckets at the ends of a pole balanced across their shoulders, depositing them into one of the 32 compartments of the waiting night soil trucks or by walking the load directly to farms to sell as fertilizer. The trucks would take the waste to plantations or to various disposal stations where, before sewage treatment systems were developed, the buckets were emptied into storm drains or rivers and then cleaned and sent back into action.

By the 1920s, Singapore began creating a proper sewage system, though night soil collection continued in a few corners of Singapore until the late 1980s. It was hard work indeed and collectors got paid very little. They had few other employment prospects due to a lack of education or ability to speak English: this job was their only option.

ORIGINAL GATE TO "THE NEW WORLD" AMUSEMENT PARK

⑥

Gateway to another world

City Square Shopping Mall
Corner of Serangoon and Kitchener Roads in Little India
MRT: Farrer Park

Leading to the gleaming City Square shopping mall in Little India is an old stone gate topped by an arch reading "The New World." It's all that remains of a colorful past. The mall was built in 2009 on the site where "The New World" amusement park once sprawled and prospered in the days when lumbering cars and buses mingled with rickshaw pullers bringing the masses (locals and Europeans alike) to the park eager to enter a world of wonder.

A Ferris wheel, roller coaster, ghost train and cinemas drew families, and so did carnival games, lucky draws and circus performances. Malay opera, Chinese puppet theater, boxing and wrestling were also popular draws. Not all of the offerings were wholesome family fare. Sexy cabaret acts titillated men and couples, as did ballroom dancing. For SGD$1, men could get three dances with a pretty young taxi-dancer (dancer for hire) in a cheongsam. Hawker stalls, snack bars and formal restaurants serving Cantonese and Western food fed customers hungry for the excitement New World offered. The park thrived for several decades before petering out in 1987.

New World was one of three amusement parks modeled after parks in Shanghai that dominated Singapore's nightlife scene in the 1920s up until the 1960s when television and shopping malls stole the show. Built in 1923 by Peranakan merchant Ong Boon Tat and his younger brother Ong Peng Hock, New World was later bought by the Shaw Brothers who also ran the Great World Amusement Park at Kim Seng Road. During Great World's heyday, the park's record attendance for one night was said to reach 50,000. Locals and British servicemen flocked there, and even foreign celebrities like Elizabeth Taylor and husband Michael Todd visited when they were in town. When the tide changed, Great World closed in 1978. Happy World (later renamed Gay World) in Geylang was the third park; it opened in 1936 and was finally shuttered in 2000, its last years a sad shadow of its former self.

During the Japanese occupation of Singapore (1942-1945), the Japanese turned all three "Worlds" parks into gambling dens for anyone who wasn't interred who wanted to try their luck. Because the Japanese taxed the gambling and made money from it, the three dens were off-limits from the aerial raids that bombarded much of the island. The dens were also off limits to Japanese soldiers.

PETAIN ROAD TOWNHOUSES

*Singapore's most outstanding examples
of the Rococo-Chinoiserie style*

Petain Road
MRT: Farrer Park

While Singapore has no short supply of vintage terrace houses and shophouses, few dazzle like the row of 18 double-story houses on off-the-beaten-track Petain Road. A riot of pattern and color hidden in plain sight amidst otherwise drab surroundings, for those in the know, these residential townhouses are considered Singapore's most outstanding examples of the Rococo-Chinoiserie style. They flaunt a flamboyant patchwork of Peranakan-style glazed ceramic tiles resplendent with floral motifs in cheerful pinks, blues and greens. The classic black and white tile walkway that fronts the entire row recalls both Chinese and English influences.

Fronting the Corinthian columns and below upper story windows, panels of ornamental plaster work also depict animals rich in traditional Chinese symbolism, from horses (symbolizing power and freedom) to birds (representing love, commitment and good fortune). Some exhibit the animal motifs in *jian nian*, a mosaic technique using porcelain pieces.

Rococo, an architectural style recognized by its over-the-top ornamentality, had been all the rage in mid-18th century Europe. Simultaneously, the West was growing enamored of all things Chinese and a decorative style known as Chinoiserie developed as a natural extension of Rococo's flair for drama.

Commissioned during the prosperous years of the Malayan rubber and tin boom a century ago, the houses were designed and built by British architects JM Jackson and his understudy EV Miller who, surprisingly, was a committed Modernist in the Bauhaus tradition of architecture, according to historian Julian Davison. These houses were built in the 1930s for landlord Mohamed bin Haji Omar, who owned a number of properties in the area.

The origin of Petain Road

In 1928, the Municipal Commission gave a number of streets in the neighborhood names to honor top World War I generals and admirals, from Kitchener to Maude, Tyrwhitt, Sturdee and Beatty. Among those was also Henri-Philippe Pétain, a French maréchal who was decorated for leading France to victory against Germany in World War I. In World War II, he collaborated with Nazi Germany and afterwards was convicted for treason and imprisoned for life. A movement to change the road's name has gained traction.

JALAN KUBOR CEMETERY

A forgotten Muslim cemetery hidden in plain sight

Kampong Glam
Intersection of Victoria and Kubor streets
Open 24/7 (there are no gates)
MRT: Lavender

Alongside the bustle of Victoria Street, groves of trees shade utter jumbles of weathered carved stones jutting this way and that amid tangles of weedy undergrowth. These are the old tombstones of some 4,000 graves of the Muslim departed, who are always buried, never burned. Curious visitors better hurry to see it, as it may disappear soon. Government authorities have earmarked this site for eventual residential development.

In 2014, historians embarked on a study of the stones here and discovered inscriptions in a veritable United Nations of scripts, including Arabic, Malay, Javanese Aksara, Bugis Aksara, Gujarati, English and Chinese. It is a testament to the vast diversity of people laid to rest here, a diversity that transcends class as well.

The cemetery is actually three separate graveyards that happened to be close to one another.

The first was once catalogued on an old map as the Tombs of the Malayan Princes by colonial architect G.D. Coleman. This section contains the burial grounds of the royal household of Sultan Hussein, but the graves here weren't limited to just royalty. In fact, so many were burying their dead here that in 1875 the government closed it down due to overcrowding and neglect. While the royal grave-markers here are larger and distinctive, none are for the Sultan himself. He and his son were both laid to rest in Malacca. The last burial here was his great-grandson, Tengku Hussain bin Tengku Haji Ali in 1954.

The second section, the Malay Burial Ground, was fenced in and well-maintained. It also has been called the Aljuneid burial ground for the large number of graves here belonging to that family, including Syed Moar and his nephew Syed Alwee bin Ali Aljuneid. And while the graveyard was closed to further burials in 1901, the Aljuneid family continued to bury family members here into the 1920s.

The third was reserved in 1848 for Indian Muslims who resided in the Kampong Glam area, who built and maintained a mosque called the Tittacheri Muslim Cemetery and mosque, located at the junction of Victoria Street and Jalan Sultan. In 1929, the Malabar Muslim Jammaat, a group that originated in India's southern state of Kerala, took it over and renamed it Masjid Malabar, *masjid* meaning "mosque" in Malay. This section of the Jalan Kubor Cemetery will be spared redevelopment, as the trustees were granted a 999-year lease in 1911.

ZUBIR SAID'S PIANO

The keys to Singapore's Nation Building

Malay Heritage Center
85 Sultan Gate
Tuesday–Sunday 10am–6pm
Free of charge to citizens and permanent residents ($4 for tourists)
MRT: Bugis

In 1958, shortly after the City Council of Singapore was inaugurated and with independence from British rule looming, Deputy Mayor Ong Pang Boon thought it was a good idea for the Council to have its own theme song and approached Zubir Said (1907–1987) to compose it.

One of the region's best-known and prolific musicians, Pak Zubir, or Uncle Zubir as he was affectionately known, scored songs and soundtracks that defined Singapore's mid-20th century golden age of cinema.

Fond of writing patriotic ditties, he was the perfect choice to write a national anthem that would mollify and unite the island's different ethnic groups as they struggled to get along in the post-war years.

Over the course of a year, Zubir composed a stately tune with simple but powerful words that resonated with the people, whether Chinese, Malay, Indian or Eurasian, and inspired them to look beyond their ethnic differences and to "let our voices soar as one."

Majulah Singapura (Onward Singapore) was written on an English-made Strohmenger grand piano at his home on Joo Chiat Road. After his death, Zubir's piano was donated to Singapore's National Heritage Board: it's currently on display at the Malay Heritage Center.

Majulah Singapura was first presented publicly on Sept. 6, 1958, as the City Council's official song. It was later to be shortened and adapted for use as the state national anthem when Singapore gained full self-government. Its debut came on Dec. 3, 1959, when Yusof bin Ishak, Singapore's first Malayan-born Yang di-Pertuan Negara (head of state), replaced the British colonial Governor. Six years later, when Singapore became independent from the Federation of Malaysia, it was formally adopted as its national anthem.

It is interesting that the man behind Singapore's national anthem was actually born in Sumatra, Indonesia. In 1928 at the age of 21, Zubir migrated to Singapore against his father's wishes and with just the shirt on his back and dreams of being a musician. In his biography, *Zubir Said, the Composer of Majulah Singapura*, his daughter Dr. Rohana Zubir writes that although he was attracted initially by Singapore's glittering lights and the luxuries of butter and coffee with milk, he was soon seduced by the opportunities Singapore offered, and his success instilled in him a strong sense of loyalty. Pak Zubir refused payment for writing the national anthem: for him it was an honor.

THE SOY SAUCE BOTTLE BOTTOMS OF THE SULTAN MOSQUE

The bottles were collected as donations from poor Muslims

Kampong Glam
3 Muscat Street
Monday–Thursday 10am–12pm and 2–4pm, Friday 2:30–4pm,
Saturday 10am–12pm and 2–4pm, closed on Sunday and public holidays
MRT: Bugis

Considered Singapore's national mosque, the Sultan Mosque resides in the country's Islamic heart, Kampong Glam, the original Muslim quarter and seat of the Malay royalty. The 1840s istana (palace) built by Sultan Ali Iskandar Shah, the eldest son of Singapore's first sultan, Sultan Hussein, still stands nearby.

The mosque's two gleaming golden onion domes, topped by pinnacles with crescent moons and stars, are a prominent site in the neighborhood and an important symbol of Singapore's Muslim heritage, both past and present. Each flanked by twin eight-story minarets, they can be seen for miles around. What is harder to spot is the band of glass bottle bottoms used as humble but striking ornamentation around the base of each dome. From a distance, they look like stripes of dark paint, but closer and in the right light, the twin necklaces of dark brown glass soy sauce bottles sparkle ever so subtly.

Completed in 1932, on the site of a previous one-story mosque sanctioned by Stamford Raffles on the request of Sultan Hussein in the early years of Colonial Singapore, the mosque was constructed in stages as funding was raised and to avoid disrupting worshippers any more than necessary. The bottles were collected as donations from poor Muslims because the mosque trustees wanted them to feel part of the community; they also wished the mosque to reflect the contributions of all Muslims, not just the wealthy.

Built by Denis Santry, an Irish architect from Swan & Maclaren, a firm responsible for designing many of Singapore's well-known Colonial-era landmarks, the mosque follows the hybrid Indo-Saracenic architectural style popular in British India at the time. It faces Mecca, which is not in keeping with the direction of the street grid, and its prayer hall holds some 5,000 worshippers. Looking refreshed after a recent restoration project, the mosque is known for being welcoming to visitors and tourists who want to have a look inside.

THE LEANING MINARET
OF HAJJAH FATIMAH MOSQUE

The Leaning Tower of Singapore

4001 Beach Road
MRT: Bugis

No, it's not your imagination, there is something askew about the Hajjah Fatimah Mosque: if you look carefully, its minaret tilts toward the main prayer hall, giving the mosque the unofficial tongue-in-cheek name "the Leaning Tower of Singapore."

The tilt began soon after construction was completed, the result of building on sandy soil. It's not a coincidence that the mosque was located on Beach Road – at the time of construction, this actually was a beach. In the 1970s, renovators attempted to correct the lean, which was worse than what can be seen today. Despite their efforts, the lean is still very evident.

The visual interest doesn't end there. Designed by a European architect, the mosque's minaret resembles the steeple of the Church of St. Andrew in Somerset, England. The prayer hall is with a dome of Indo-Saracenic flavor and a Moorish wooden balcony tops the entrance. In the 1930s, French contractors, Chinese architects and Malay craftsmen rebuilt the prayer hall. The result is a charming multi-cultural East-meets-West mashup, from the Doric capitals topping European-style columns to the green glazed ceramic roof tiles imported from China and the delicately-hand-carved wooden Malay ornamentation.

The first mosque in Singapore to be named after a woman

Hajjah Fatimah (*hajjah* being an honorific title bestowed on a Muslim woman who has made the pilgrimage to Mecca) was a wealthy widow who turned her deceased husband's trading business into a smashing success. Her house was originally located at this site, but had been twice burgled. During the second break-in, it was set on fire. Thankful to Allah for sparing her life, she built this mosque out of gratitude in 1846. Eventually, the mosque would bear her name, the first mosque in Singapore to be named after a woman – very few are. Upon her passing at the age of 98, she was interred in a private chamber located at the back of the mosque. Hajjah Fatimah Mosque became a National Monument in 1973.

GASHOLDER FRAME

The last remain of the historic Kallang Gas Works

Kallang Gasworks
Kallang Riverside Park
MRT: Kallang

A curious circle of pillars at Kallang Riverside Park looks like it could be just another part of the urban park infrastructure, a sort of giant topless open-air gazebo. But this steam-punk fairy ring is actually what remains of an industrial revolution-era landmark that once occupied this site. The eight pillars and connecting girders were the support structure for Gas Holder No. 3, a steel cylindrical tank that was used for storing gas.

They are all that remains of the Kallang Gas Works, and belonged to one of four gas holders. Built in 1862 by the Singapore Gas Company, the plant converted coal into gas that was piped out to fuel street lamps, the first facility of its kind in Singapore. Hokkiens knew it as *huay sia*, which meant "fire city," out of fear that the plant could explode at any moment. This probably explains why the facility was guarded round the clock by Gurkhas, soldiers of Nepalese descent known for their military might.

Over the years, Kallang Gas Works underwent many changes. As electricity gradually took over the job of lighting city streets – Singapore's last gas street lamp was extinguished in 1956 – gas lines were diverted to homes for cooking and heating water. Coal was also replaced as the main fuel source, changed out for heavy fuel oil and naphtha, a flammable mixture of liquid hydrocarbon.

Kallang Gas Works was decommissioned in 1998, after over 130 years of service. Near the gas holder frame, a public artwork, *The Spirit of Kallang*, was crafted by local sculptor Lim Leong Seng out of pipes and gauges from the original plant.

Communal riots of 1964

On July 21, 1964, violence broke out in the vicinity of Kallang Gas Works between a Muslim procession celebrating the Prophet Mohammed's birthday and Chinese bystanders, sparking an island-wide riot that killed four people and injured 178 others in the first day alone. The riots took place amid a backdrop of rising political tensions between Singapore's People's Action Party (PAP) and Malaysia's United Malays National Organisation (UMNO) following the formation of a unified Malaysia that included Singapore (Singapore remained a part of Malaysia for less than two years, from 1963–1965). In total, 36 people died from riots that summer and autumn. Since 1997, Singapore has celebrated Racial Harmony Day every July 21.

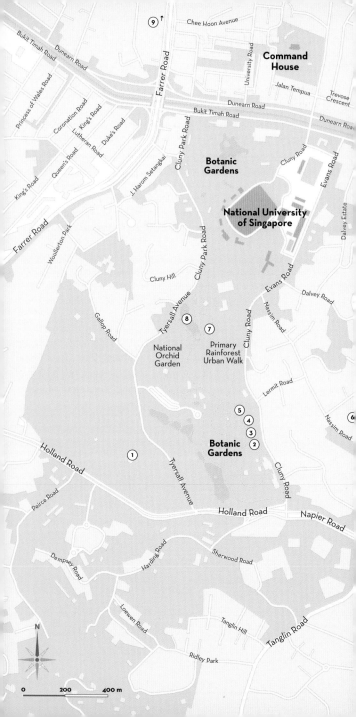

⑨ ↑

Chee Hoon Avenue

Command House

Bukit Timah Road

Dunearn Road

Princess of Wales Road

Coronation Road

King's Road

Lutheran Road

Duke's Road

University Road

Jalan Tempua

Trevose Crescent

Dunearn Road

Bukit Timah Road

Dunearn Road

Farrer Road

Cluny Park Road

King's Road

Queen's Road

Farrer Road

Woollerton Park

Gallop Road

Cluny Hill

J. Harom Setangkai

Cluny Park Road

Botanic Gardens

National University of Singapore

Cluny Road

Evans Road

Dalvey Estate

Evans Road

Dalvey Road

Cluny Road

Nassim Road

Tyersall Avenue

⑧

⑦

Primary Rainforest Urban Walk

National Orchid Garden

Lermit Road

Nassim Road

⑤

④

③

②

⑥

Botanic Gardens

Holland Road

Peirce Road

Tyersall Avenue

Holland Road

Napier Road

Dempsey Road

Harding Road

Sherwood Road

Loewen Road

Tanglin Hill

Tanglin Road

Ridley Park

N

0   200   400 m

Botanic Gardens and Environs

1. ISTANA WOODNEUK — 138
2. LIBRARY OF BOTANY AND HORTICULTURE — 140
3. SINGAPORE BOTANIC GARDENS' TIGER ORCHID — 141
4. ARROWS ON BRICKS — 142
5. *GIRL ON A SWING* SCULPTURE — 144
6. THE FLAGPOLE OF "EDEN HALL" — 146
7. A STUMP-UMENT TO SINGAPORE'S FIRST RUBBER TREE — 148
8. WOODEN ARROW — 150
9. WWII POW CALENDAR — 152

ISTANA WOODNEUK

Singapore's other royal palace

Between Holland Road and Tyersall Avenue
MRT: Botanic Gardens

Hidden atop a jungly hillock off busy Holland Road, just off the southern end of the Botanic Gardens, are the ruins of an old Malay royal "mansion", Woodneuk House. All that can now be seen are its walls, pretty wrought iron balcony railings, carved ventilation panels and streamline Modernist window sun-shade fins, leaving its past grandeur to the imagination. The only decorations of its once richly furnished rooms are the vines and plants that have taken root. Strewn all around with litter and debris are shards of the blue ceramic tiles that once covered its roof. In the rooms, the who's who of early 20th-century Singapore would once have mingled at elegant dinners and cocktail parties, sipping champagne from lead crystal and gazing out over manicured lawns that reached across to the Singapore Botanic Gardens' Swan Lake.

The very first Woodneuk was built in 1861, possibly by William MacDonald, whose diverse businesses included property, shipping and insurance, Woodneuk was let out to a number of prominent people. One, Captain John Ross, a famous trader, shipper and explorer, eventually acquired the house. Ross's son, John Dill, described the house in much detail in a 1911 book, *Sixty Years: Life and Adventure in the Far East*, in which he referred to it as 'Woodleigh.'

Sultan Abu Bakar of Johor (1833–1895) added the estate to his neighboring Tyersall Palace, which he built in place of a house built by lawyer and publisher William Napier (after whom a nearby road is named). On Abu Bakar's death, the two-house property passed on to Sultan Ibrahim (1873–1959), Abu Bakar's heir. Ibrahim showed a preference for Woodneuk over the larger and more formal Tyersall. A disastrous fire destroyed Tyersall in 1905 after which Woodneuk became the Sultan's official Singapore residence.

Sultan Ibrahim rebuilt Woodneuk between 1932 and 1935 for the third of his four official wives, a Scot named Helen Bartholomew (1889–1978). The couple divorced in 1938. The Japanese Occupation saw Woodneuk used as a military hospital. The end of the war brought several bigwigs as residents: two successive Commanders-in-Chief, Sir Miles Dempsey and Sir Montagu Stopford, and Malcolm MacDonald, a Governor-General.

In the late 1940s, Woodneuk was renovated and again served as the Sultan's Singapore residence. A stunning blue-tiled roof, which was completely destroyed by fire in 2006, was installed in 1952. Abandoned in the 1960s, even if it remained in the Johor royal family's possession, Woodneuk was soon swallowed up by the surrounding jungle and now lies forgotten by all but a few intrepid explorers.

LIBRARY OF BOTANY AND HORTICULTURE

A botanical bible

Singapore Botanic Gardens
1 Cluny Road
MRT: Botanic Gardens

English botanist Isaac Henry Burkill (1870–1965) succeeded Henry Ridley as the second Director of the Singapore Botanic Gardens (SBG) in 1912. He retired from this post at the age of 55 in 1925 and spent the next decade researching and compiling the encyclopedic *Dictionary of the Economic Products of the Malay Peninsula*. In the 2,400-page, two-volume *Dictionary*, Burkill describes 4,656 species from 1,630 genera of plants in 223 families, and  includes vernacular names as well. One of the most comprehensive texts on the historical uses of tropical plants, it's considered indispensible to any economist or historian writing about Malaya. "It's still an important source of reference, in fact there is no other that is not derived from it," says Dr. Nigel Taylor, director of the SBG from 2011-2019. Burkill's *magnum opus* was reprinted in 1966 and if you ask the staff, you can leaf through the books in the SBG Library of Botany and Horticulture.

Plantation Nation: Burkill Hall

Set at the highest point in the SBG on the far edges of the National Orchid Garden, Burkill Hall, built in 1868, is the last surviving example of the early Anglo-Malayan plantation-style bungalow in Malaysia and Singapore. In its early years, the SBG was in fact like an enormous plantation, filled with nutmeg and rubber trees. Not a classic Singapore "black and white" house, its very broad overhanging roof provides generous shade from the tropical sun, and the *porte cochère* entrance and second-floor verandah were typical design features of 19th-century plantation houses. Burkill Hall was built as the home for the Gardens' first superintendent, Laurence Niven (1826-1876), and all subsequent directors up till Richard E. Holttum lived there. In 1992, the building was restored and renamed Burkill Hall in honor of Burkill and his son, Humphrey Morrison Burkill (1914–2006), who was also a director of SBG, from 1957 to 1969.

SINGAPORE BOTANIC GARDENS' ③ TIGER ORCHID

The world's oldest and largest

1 Cluny Road
Junction of Singapore Botanic Gardens' Main Gate Road and the pergola of
hanging vines (known as the Curtain of Roots)
Daily 5am–midnight
MRT: Botanic Garden

Strollers and joggers padding along Main Gate Road inside Singapore Botanic Gardens (SBG) pass by a big, green, unruly mass daily, having no clue about the position it holds in the botanical world.

In 1861, the first director of Singapore Botanic Gardens, Lawrence Niven, planted a tiger orchid at the intersection of two paths, near today's Curtain of Roots, a pergola hosting a long fringe of aerial roots. Still growing in the same spot after all these years, the now giant 5-meter-wide orchid is believed to be the world's oldest and largest. The massive green clump profusely flowers once every year or two after a period of dry weather, with inflorescences (flowering stems) as long as two-to-three meters supporting dozens of golden and deep-purple speckled flowers. When not in bloom, the innocuous mound of wayward green-ness goes unnoticed.

For its own protection, a few years ago a fence was put up around the tiger orchid to contain the old beast within. It's a symbolic reminder that wild tigers roamed around 19th-century Singapore and that, in the late 1800s, the SBG developed a zoo that included tigers in cages (it closed in 1905).

The huge, caged tiger orchid is believed to be a wild Singaporean specimen. It's an interesting scientific development considering that, until recently, the wild tiger orchid had been widely considered extinct for nearly a century.

The SBG has been a pioneer in developing innovative orchid breeding techniques that have fostered Singapore's thriving orchid industry since the 1920s when the SBG director, Prof. Eric Holttum, started orchid hybridization and seed germination programs. The result is the SBG has registered more than 600 orchid hybrids.

ARROWS ON BRICKS

An act of defiance by POWs in WWII

Singapore Botanic Gardens
1 Cluny Road
MRT: Botanical Gardens

Millions of feet have trampled on the innocuous-looking red brick steps near the Plant House of the Singapore Botanic Gardens (SBG), but few people look down to notice the little arrows etched into many of them.

The bricks used for these steps were made by Australian Prisoners of War (POWs) in Changi Prison during the Japanese Occupation of Singapore between 1942 and 1945. During those three years, the Japanese took control of the Botanic Gardens and appointed renowned Japanese botanist Kwan Koriba as its director. Koriba retained the SBG's former staff, including British officers and scientists Richard Holttum and EJH Corner, who before the war had been the SBG's director and assistant director, respectively. The Japanese took great pains to keep the Gardens well-maintained for they saw it as a valuable resource for the global Empire they hoped to grow and sustain.

While the Japanese treated the Gardens and the Raffles Museum and Library with tender loving care, it was a different story for the POWs under their command. The Japanese were brutal captors, providing little food and water to the men they forced into hard labor in the tropical sun. To feel a shred of control in their otherwise wretched existence, the POWS assigned to make the bricks decided to etch little arrows onto the bricks before firing them as a type of silent protest that the Japanese would not have understood. In Singapore, arrows were routinely used to mark government property and survey points, and serve the same purpose today. You can see them pressed into sidewalks and driveways all over the island.

For decades the markings went undetected. Then, in August 1995, a group of eight elderly Australian former World War II POWs visited the Gardens and asked to be taken to the Plant House. They were shocked and very excited to see the bricks they had made and installed were still intact. Their memories came flooding back and the men shared the story about their subversive arrow making and the mark they left on Singapore's history.

GIRL ON A SWING SCULPTURE

⑤

Dedicated to the children of Singapore

Singapore Botanic Garden
Tanglin Gate at Cluny and Napier Roads
5am–midnight
Free
MRT: Botanic Garden

Just above a hedge in the middle of the Singapore Botanic Gardens near the old Bandstand gazebo, a young girl floats joyously on a swing that appears to hang in thin air. This winsome and nearly-camouflaged bronze sculpture, called *Girl on a Swing*, is by well-known British sculptor Sydney Harpley (1927–1992).

The work was commissioned by David Saul Marshall (1908–1995), Singapore's first Chief Minister and Ambassador to France. Marshall, who was also Singapore's greatest criminal and constitutional lawyer, fell in love with Harpley's work and commissioned the sculpture, insisting that the artist depict a Malay, rather than a European girl on the swing. Marshall sent Harpley more than 30 photographs of a young Malay factory worker to give him an idea of what he had in mind. The result is the smiling, barefoot girl in a traditional *sarong kebaya*, swinging happily through the air. Completed in 1984, *Girl on a Swing* was the first of three sculptures commissioned by Marshall and donated to the Singapore Botanic Gardens. All three sculptures – the other two being *Girl on a Bicycle* and *Lady in a Hammock* – are dedicated to the children of Singapore and have been installed in the gardens.

Although Marshall commissioned *Girl on a Swing* at the cost of SG$30,000, Harpley retained the right to produce up to six identical copies of the work. *Girl on a Bicycle* was not a commissioned work. It was sculptured by Harpley and first exhibited in 1977. The piece installed at the Botanic Gardens was the last of seven identical sculptures cast from the same mould and was to have been sold to an art dealer when Marshall persuaded Harpley to sell it to him. He donated it to the Gardens in 1987. *Lady in a Hammock* had originally been sculpted in 1981 and was known as *Nude in a Hammock*. Marshall bequeathed the sculpture to the Botanic Gardens in 1989. The Harpley sculptures were the first to be donated and installed in the Botanic Gardens, which was declared a UNESCO World Heritage site in 2015.

THE FLAGPOLE OF "EDEN HALL"

May the Union Jack fly here forever

28 Nassim Road
MRT: Botanic Gardens

Since 1957, when the 1904-built Eden Hall was sold to the British government, a flagpole in the front lawn has towered over a small plaque at its base that reads: "May the Union Jack fly here forever." And indeed, since then, Eden Hall has been the residence of successive UK representatives in Singapore and, since 1965, of the High Commissioner.

Before the Edwardian-style two-story mansion, often called the "Wedding Cake" and "Wedgwood House" because of its frilly white

plasterwork, passed into the hands of the British, it was the property of Baghdadi Jewish businessman Ezekiel Saleh Manasseh. The wealthy merchant made his fortune in the rice and opium trades and built the grand 14,000-square-foot mansion on posh Nassim Road on a former nutmeg plantantion; he had his initial "M" fashioned into the spindles of Eden Hall's interior wrought-iron balustrade.

The mansion was designed by British Architect R.A.J. Bidwell of Swan & Maclaren, a local firm responsible for many prominent Singapore properties during the Colonial years. Bidwell would have been used to Singapore's rich and famous wanting to brand their properties with their initials. Manasseh Meyer, for instance, also asked Bidwell to have "M's" worked into some interior railings of his Chesed-El synagogue (see page 98).

After renting it out for a time, in 1916, Manasseh moved in with his bride, an English widow named Elsie Trilby Bath and her two children. Her son Vivian attended school in Australia and England, then returned to Eden Hall and started working for a Singapore rubber-brokerage firm. He enjoyed his life as a wealthy hobnobbing expatriate until WWII broke out and the party was over. Vivian joined the Singapore Volunteer Forces, and after the Fall of Singapore was shipped off to a labor camp in Hokkaido, Japan. His stepfather, Manasseh, was interned in Changi Prison and died in the prison hospital on Sime Road.

During the Japanese Occupation, Eden Hall was used by the Japanese as an officers' mess and fortunately was well looked after. When Vivian returned to Singapore after the war, he regained possession of the house and, before retiring to Australia, sold it to the British government for 56,000 pounds, a fraction of what the mansion on tony Nassim Road could fetch today.

A STUMP-UMENT TO SINGAPORE'S FIRST RUBBER TREE

Where the first rubber tree in Singapore was planted in 1877

Singapore Botanic Gardens (SBG)
1 Cluny Road, Tanglin Gate entrance
MRT: Botanic Gardens

Behind Symphony Stage, near clumps of flowering *Heliconia* plants at the center of the Singapore Botanic Gardens (SBG), a chunky stump-shaped monument marks the spot where the first rubber tree in Singapore was planted in 1877. While that actual tree no longer survives, there are third-generation rubber trees growing nearby, close to the SBG's Botany Centre.

Before rubber trees were grown in the Far East, one had to make the long journey to Brazil to tap latex from wild ones. When Scottish chemist Charles Macintosh patented a method for making waterproof garments in 1823, leading to the invention of the raincoat and a host of other valuable products, British and European businessmen were

champing at the bit to harvest rubber closer to home. In 1876, English explorer Henry Wickham stepped up to the challenge and smuggled 7,000 rubber saplings out of Brazil in bundles of wool wrapped with banana leaves, and into England to Kew Gardens.

Saplings were grown in the Royal Botanical Garden in London and sent to British colonies all over the world, including 22 bound for Singapore and Malaya (as Malaysia was known in those days). Of those, 11 were planted at the SBG in 1877. With a tropical climate like the Amazon, rubber trees thrived in Singapore.

Rubber-obsessed Ridley

When Henry Ridley (1855–1956) arrived in Singapore in 1888 to assume the directorship of the Botanic Gardens, there were some 1,100 rubber trees in the SBG, but there was no interest in cultivating rubber commercially. The single-minded Ridley made it a personal mission to encourage local and European planters to grow rubber, thrusting rubber seeds into the hands of anyone half likely to accept them. Not suprisingly, he was known as "Mad Ridley" or "Rubber Ridley." By 1896, the first plantations in Malaya were growing rubber trees and by 1910 the rubber was ready for market. Perfect timing: thanks to the mass production of cars in the early 20th century, Malaya became the world's top rubber producer, a lofty title it held for years. SBG Director (2011-2019) Dr. Nigel Taylor estimates that about 70 per cent of all rubber latex harvested in the world today originates in Southeast Asia and those 11 rubber trees planted in the SBG way back when.

Tree tapping genius

More important than Ridley's zealous promotion of rubber-growing was his method for tapping the trees for their sticky latex, which would be turned into sheet rubber. Ridley's 'herringbone technique' allowed rubber trees to be tapped almost daily without serious harm to the tree, and it's still used today. Several streets near the SBG are named after him.

WOODEN ARROW

The spot where the earth's terrestrial magnetism was measured in 1914

Singapore Botanic Gardens
Symphony Lake, Lat. 1789 N and longitude 103.48
MRT: Botanic Gardens

I n the middle of Symphony Lake in the Singapore Botanic Gardens (SBG), a simple wooden arrow atop a tall, thin post appears to be pointing at a bunch of trees. In fact, it's aiming north towards Greenwich, in London, England: the arrow marks the spot where the earth's terrestrial magnetism was measured in 1914 by teams of scientists from the Royal Greenwich Observatory of England and the Carnegie Institution for Science in Washington DC, USA.

It was marked so the researchers could return again to take measurements of this important characteristic. The earth's magnetic field, which emanates from the earth's core out into the atmosphere, acts like a shield protecting the planet from harsh solar winds and cosmic radiation. We couldn't live without it.

Originally, the wooden arrow was a stone marker set amid rows of various plants in a nursery that existed there on dry land, before Symphony Lake was created in 1976. Today the arrow appears to be utterly lost in its aquatic home.

Profit-making gardens

While today the SBG is considered a beautiful peaceful green place to walk your dog, go jogging or have a picnic with family and friends, in the beginning, the SBG was created first and foremost as a research facility and a commercial enterprise where ideas were germinated and grown into revenue-generating businesses. The SBG has been particularly successful at orchid breeding and the rubber boom in Malaya and Singapore a century ago all started in the SBG. The first seedlings brought to Southeast Asia from England were planted in the SBG in 1877 and a few decades later started producing latex. The rest is history.

WWII POW CALENDAR

A map of Singapore scrawled with dates buried underneath layers of paint

Wall of Black & White House
No. 5 Adam Park
MRT: Botanic Gardens

Imagine scraping paint off a guest room wall in preparation for a fresh coat, only to find a message from the past, from prisoners of war who were interned there decades before.

Such was the fate of the resident at No. 5 Adam Park, who was renting the black and white bungalow from the government. A map of Singapore

scrawled with dates was found buried underneath layers of paint.

Singapore's black and white houses were built to house military officers during colonial times, but few know that they also housed Allied Prisoners of War. Their story is unraveling through the efforts of The Adam Park Project, the first comprehensive archaeological survey of a Singapore WWII battlefield and POW camp. The project has uncovered many details about the lives of the prisoners here, including the calendar.

Written in pencil, the dates on the calendar span from September to December 1942 and were believed to have been written by a member of the Australian 8th Division Signals who were housed at this bungalow. According to researchers, the calendar counts down the days until the POWs would be paid for their work on the Syonan Jinja Shrine at nearby MacRitchie Reservoir. Each POW was paid 10 cents a day, every 14 days.

Another POW mural

The Adam Park project has also uncovered painted wall murals at No. 11 Adam Park, which was the site of the POW's Chapel, the second such chapel in Singapore after the Changi Prison Chapel. It was on the second floor above the camp's canteen where Capt. Eric Andrews built the chapel, repairing parts of the house that had been blown out, and painted, among other murals, an image of Mary Magdalene rolling back the rock that closed the tomb in which Jesus was laid to rest. In place of her face, Capt. Andrews pasted the face of American actress Dorothy Lamour that had been cut out from a magazine. Work is currently underway to determine how many murals still exist on the walls here.

In all, the POWs spent from March 1942 to January 1943 in the camp. Adam Park had been the site of a fierce battle, but afterwards held about 2,000 Australian and 1,000 British prisoners. Those who survived the ordeal were later marched to Changi or sent by train up to Thailand to work on the Thai-Burma Railway, where many died from starvation and disease. Battlefield archaeologist Jon Cooper spent years in Singapore digging around Adam Park; he and his volunteers dug up more than 1,000 relics that helped tell the story of the WWII battles that raged here and lives of the POWs corralled into the Adam Park camps. Cooper founded the virtual museum, the AdamParkProject.com, in a continuing effort to preserve this chapter in Singapore history.

Bukit Timah, Southern Coast, Jurong and North

1. THE PIER AT LIM CHU KANG — 156
2. WOODLANDS JETTY — 158
3. KAMPUNG ADMIRALTY ROOFTOP — 160
4. SEMBAWANG HOT SPRINGS — 162
5. SYONAN JINJA SHRINE — 164
6. BUKIT TIMAH SUMMIT — 166
7. BOARDROOM AT THE FORMER FORD FACTORY — 168
8. LITTLE GUILIN — 170
9. NANTAH ARCH — 172
10. GARDEN OF FAME — 174
11. MACHINE-GUN PILLBOX — 176
12. THE ORIGINAL STEPS TO HAW PAR VILLA — 178
13. THE GAP — 180
14. YING FO FUI KUN CEMETERY — 182
15. THE PLAQUE OF ALEXANDRA HOSPITAL — 184
16. FORMER BREWMASTER'S HOUSE — 186
17. FULLERTON HOTEL LIGHTHOUSE BEACON — 188
18. WHITE OBELISK AT LABRADOR PARK — 190
19. A WARTIME JAPANESE GRAVE — 192
20. HARBOURFRONT 19TH-CENTURY STEAM CRANE — 194
21. FORT IMBIAH BATTERY — 196
22. SENTOSA BOARDWALK — 198
23. THE TOWERS OF LIGHTS SEEN FROM GHOST ISLAND — 200
24. RAFFLES LIGHTHOUSE — 202

THE PIER AT LIM CHU KANG

A weekend escape for a wealthy family

Lim Chu Kang Road end
MRT: Choa Chu Kang to Bus 975 to the Police Coast Guard (34009)

The Pier is a century-old seaside pavilion built on a jetty that extends out over the mudflats in remote northwest Singapore at the edge of a mangrove forest. Best viewed from the end of Lim Chu Kang Road, it was an escape like none other for the wealthy Cashin family and was one of several residences the family owned.

While the sea pavilion dates to the 1920s, the structure on which it rests goes back further to 1906. As its name would suggest, its original purpose was that of a boat landing point, intended to allow rubber to be moved by sea from Alexander William Cashin's estate to Kranji, also along Singapore's northern coast. From Kranji, the goods could be moved by road to the port in Singapore's south. Rubber cultivation, introduced to Singapore in the late 1880s, dominated much of Singapore's rural landscape by the turn of the century and this included the isolated northwest.

When the pier became obsolete with the establishment of land transport links, Cashin built a pavilion on the end of it as a seaside getaway. It became the home of Cashin's son, Howard, in the 1960s, when the younger Cashin moved in with his wife, living in it until his passing in 2009. It was then transferred to the State and, after being vacant for several years, it is now being made into a visitor center for a new western entrance into the bird-rich grounds of the Sungei Buloh Wetland Reserve.

Not occupying a particularly scenic spot, its attraction is found perhaps in its isolation, and in the views it provides over and across the narrow western Johor Strait separating Singapore from Malaysia. The Pier's most distinguished visitor, Sultan Ismail of Johor, would boat over from Malaysia. The grandfather of the current sultan, he would often come to have tea with the Cashins. These visits recall times when borders meant little and when the Orang Seletar, a tribe of boat-dwelling people who inhabited the strait, crossed at will on their houseboats.

The beginning of the end

It was also from across the waterway that the first invading troops of the Japanese Imperial Army's 5th Division during World War II came on a dark and fateful February night in 1942. A valiant but vain effort was mounted by the Australian 22nd Brigade in defense of the grounds of The Pier. Some 360 troops are estimated to have fallen in a prelude to Britain's "greatest capitulation" just a week later.

WOODLANDS JETTY

One of the best places in Singapore to catch smoldering sunsets

Woodlands Waterfront Park
Bus 856 from MRT: Yishun – After RMN Barracks Stop (47019)
Bus 856 from MRT: Woodlands – Before RMN Barracks Stop (47011)

None of the other parks in all of Singapore has what the 27-acre Woodlands Waterfront Park along Singapore's northern coast has: a big long L-shaped jetty measuring 36 feet across that's open to the public.

The fishermen know it; anglers always seem to be hanging out there hoping for a nibble. It's also a popular spot for savvy strollers who know the jetty is one of the best places in Singapore to catch beautiful sunsets, not to mention sweeping views of the coastline and the Straits of Johor. Malaysia's southernmost city Johor Bahru is just across the Causeway.

Part of the Royal Malaysian Navy until 1997

Built in 1966, the jetty was not always used for recreation. Occupying a spot within the British Admiralty's huge naval base, the jetty provided berthing space for ships flying the naval ensign – not of a newly independent Singapore, or of Britain, but of Malaysia, the country across the strait. Hard as it is to imagine such an arrangement, especially given the relationship between the two countries, the jetty was a component of the main naval base of the Royal Malaysian Navy (RMN).

Known first as HMS Malaya, and at the time of the jetty's construction, as KD Malaya, the siting of the base owes much to the two countries' shared history. Formed as the Malayan Naval Force (MNF) in 1949, the designated site inside Britain's own naval base made perfect sense. Singapore, even if it was then governed as a separate entity, had always been seen as part of a greater Malaya. The MNF became the Royal Malayan Navy in 1952, and the Royal Malaysian Navy when Singapore merged with Malaya to form Malaysia in 1963. The marriage between Singapore and Malaysia did not last long and, in August 1965, the two separated.

The Separation Agreement permitted Malaysia to retain its military facilities in Singapore. RMN would use Woodlands as its main base until 1979 when a new base in Lumut in the north of Malaysia was completed. However, the RMN did not vacate the base at that juncture, using it until December 1997, after which it was handed over to Singapore. Parts of the former KD Malaya were later developed as Woodlands Waterfront Park, which opened in May 2010.

KAMPUNG ADMIRALTY ROOFTOP ③

Hidden layers of lushness

676 Woodlands Drive 71
Daily 6am–10pm
Free
MRT: Admiralty

While almost all of Singapore's rural *kampung* villages have been razed to make way for urban development, one particular city block has been ingeniously designed to incorporate some of the best aspects of *kampung* living.

Out of sight from the hustle and bustle of city streets, the upper levels of Kampung Admiralty open up to a glorious rooftop – a "vertical *kampung*"

as some people like to name it. The rooftop reproduces in fact the idea of a vertical communal village landscaped with trees, shrubs and lush greenery on multiple levels that are layered like stepped hillside terraces.

It's a stroke of architectural inspiration, as this particular block was designed specifically for elderly residents, who would remember *kampung* life and derive deep nostalgic meaning from a close proximity to the botanical surroundings.

For the residents' pleasure, the gardens contain a communal farm and orchard laden with local varieties of fruits, vegetables and herbs, as well as park fixtures that encourage elderly residents of Kampung Admiralty's 104 apartments to spend time outdoors amid nature and community. All this on an urban block that measures just under 2 ½ acres.

The genius of Kampung Admiralty doesn't end there – the entire block is an experiment in designing urban communities for an ageing population. While the upper levels support elderly-friendly housing and community gardens, lower levels house a large covered open-air plaza for community and public activities, including a specialist outpatient medical center with waiting areas that face the gardens, shops and a hawker center. There's also an "Active Ageing Hub" with co-located day care facilities for seniors and young children.

Completed in 2017, Kampung Admiralty was designed by Singapore-based Woha Architects, a firm that has received international acclaim for designs that incorporate nature and sustainability.

Unlike most buildings, Kampung Admiralty came to be through the cooperation of not just a few government agencies, but many bodies, including Singapore's Housing & Development Board (HDB), Ministry of Health (MOH), Yishun Health Campus (YHC), National Environment Agency (NEA), National Parks Board (NParks), Land Transport Authority (LTA) and Early Childhood Development Agency (ECDA).

Building of the Year 2018
In 2018, Kampung Admiralty clinched Building of the Year at the prestigious World Architectural Festival.

SEMBAWANG HOT SPRINGS

Singapore's only thermal springs, hidden inside a military facility

Sembawang Military Base
Gambas Avenue
Daily 7am–7pm
Free
MRT: Yishun to Bus 858 or 969, opp Blk 115B (57121)

If Singapore's weather isn't hot and steamy enough, an even steamier experience awaits in Sembawang. The northern suburb is where the only thermal springs on the main island, the Sembawang Hot Springs, can be found hidden in a military facility.

The springs' sulfur-rich waters are valued by folks seeking to alleviate skin and rheumatic conditions. The military authorities allow public access to the site during daylight hours, and recently the area was spruced up and is now called the Sembawang Hot Spring Park.

A gate in the facility's northern boundary at Gambas Avenue opens to a pathway to the springs. It is at the end of this path that one will realize that the springs are not quite out of a picture book. The springs' flows are instead controlled, in a most Singaporean-like manner, through taps. Pails are used to collect the flow and even with the strong

whiff of rotten eggs from the flows, you will usually find quite a few folks soaking their feet. Some also actually bring eggs, which are left in containers and placed under the taps to slowly cook.

The springs were discovered in 1908 on land belonging to Seah Eng Keong. Seah's father, Seah Eu Chin, was a well-known merchant and the founder of the Ngee Ann Kongsi (a clan association) that cultivated gambier and pepper in the area. An equally enterprising younger Seah had the water bottled before Fraser and Neave (F&N) – a well-known local bottler – bought the springs in 1921. Bottling was disrupted by the war. The Japanese, known for their fondness for thermal baths, used the springs in that manner until Allied bombing in November 1941 halted the flow. It was only in 1967 that F&N re-started bottling under the Seletaris brand. In the mid-1980s the land was acquired by the government.

A condominium named Seletaris now sits on the site of the former bottling plant, just across the road from the springs. The springs itself became part of a military base in the 1990s. Local residents used the abandoned springs in the interim and put in requests to be allowed into the site. Acceding to their thirst for entry, military authorities have allowed the public in since 2002.

In late 2018, a development project added some new features to the hot springs area, including a cascading pool, wheelchair accessibility and more trees in a park-like environment.

'Toilet water'

Seah Eng Keong bottled the water under various names, including "Zombun water" or "Air Zombun." In Malay, this sounded similar to "air jamban," meaning "toilet water," and as you can imagine, quickly became a source of many a joke.

SYONAN JINJA SHRINE ⑤

A shinto shrine built in the jungle by POWs

MacRitchie Reservoir Park
GPS coordinates N 01' 20.900 E 103' 48.820
MRT: Caldecott

As fierce as the Japanese were as soldiers and captors, they were equally as intense in their reverence for nature and their ancient Shinto faith, a belief system based on seeking a balance between nature, humans and the divine.

At the start of the Japanese occupation of Singapore (1942-1945), thousands of British and Australian prisoners of war were put to work on building projects in Singapore, Burma, Thailand, Borneo and Japan. One project at home was the Syonan Jinja – the "Light of the South Shinto" shrine. The Shrine was built atop a forested hill along the far western edge of the MacRitchie Reservoir, near Sime and Adam roads, where the most intense fighting in Japan's battle for Singapore had taken place.

Its design was inspired by the Ise Grand Shrine in Japan, admired for its natural setting and simplistic architecture. Used mainly by the Japanese, Syonan Jinja was opened on the first anniversary of the fall of Singapore in February 1943. Locals in Singapore were sometimes

compelled to attend public ceremonies there to show their respect.

As the end of the war loomed in 1945 and with the British poised to take back Singapore, the Japanese destroyed as much of the Syonan Jinja as they could. The wooden structures and many traditional Torii gates were burned, but much of the stone parts have survived. Hidden deep in the thick jungle and enveloped by trees, fronds and moss, a trough-like stone font was used for ritual purification before prayer. A good portion of the raised platform upon which the font is set, and a second higher platform, peeks through the overgrown foliage. A grand set of stairs leading to the base of the shrine also remains in remarkably good condition, protected by nature all of these years.

When water levels are low, you can still see the wooden stubs of the supports that once held up the Divine Bridge, a span across the reservoir that led to a point near the foot of the shrine where a large Torii gate once stood.

At the same time the Syonan Jinja was being built, two war memorials dedicated to the war dead also were being constructed nearby at the peak of Bukit Batok – one for the British and the Syonan Chureito for the Japanese. After the war, the remains of Japanese dead were moved to the Japanese cemetery on Chuan Hoe Avenue (no British were ever buried there). The memorials were destroyed, except for the stairs leading up to the monuments' platform.

BUKIT TIMAH SUMMIT

Highest point in Singapore

Bukit Timah Summit
Hindhede Drive, off of Bukit Timah Road
MRT: Beauty World

Trekkers who make the journey to the summit of the nearly 537-foot tall Bukit Timah Hill may not realize they've scaled Singapore's highest natural point, unless that is, they notice the stone marker near a few SingTel telecommunications towers. Sadly, there are no rewarding vistas as the dense vegetation of the surrounding forest blocks any potential views. Still, as home to Singapore's only remaining primary rainforest, and one of only a few cities in the world with rainforest hugging its outskirts, hiking around Bukit Timah Nature Reserve is a worthwhile endeavor.

For a better view

The Pinnacle@Duxton is nearly as tall as Bukit Timah but its urban location offers far better views. The world's tallest public housing building also has the longest sky gardens (just over 1,640 feet long), located at the building's 50th floor. It is open to the public, but off the typical tourist path (see page 24). An EZ-Link card is needed for access; get one at most MRT stations, 7-Eleven shops or Shell petrol kiosks.

Singapore's tallest building is the Tanjong Pagar Centre, also called the Guoco Building Tower, at nearly 952 feet, some 415 feet taller than Bukit Timah Hill.

BOARDROOM AT THE FORMER FORD FACTORY

Where fortress Singapore surrendered

351 Upper Bukit Timah Road
www.nas.gov.sg/formerfordfactory/exhibition
Monday–Saturday 9am–5:30pm, Sunday noon–5:30pm
English Tours: Monday–Friday 2:30pm, Saturday 11am–3:30pm, Sunday
2:30pm and 3:30pm
Mandarin Tours: on selected Saturdays; check the dates and times on the
website
Buses 75, 171, 178 or 961 from MRT: Hillview

In its quiet and modern residential surroundings, the former Ford Factory, with its Art Deco-style façade, seems out of place. Built as the Ford Motor Company of Malaya's plant for the assembly of automobiles, its completion in 1941 seemed timely – the factory was put to immediate use in support of the war effort.

The impact, however, did little to change the course the war was taking and in less than a year the factory would be caught up in an event that changed the course of history – the February 15, 1942 surrender of Singapore to the Japanese.

It is perhaps apt that the building, at which the assembly of motor vehicles long ago ceased, is a permanent site for an exhibition in which the dark days that followed the event are remembered. Also remembered is the surrender itself in the very boardroom at which Gen. Arthur Percival faced off with Gen. Tomoyuki Yamashita and agreed to the unconditional surrender of Singapore. A projection of the room, furnished as it would then have been, is taken from a widely circulated photograph of the surrender in which the main protagonists are depicted at that fateful moment. A wall clock freezes time at 6.20pm, the moment when whatever illusions the British Empire held of its invincibility, evaporated.

In other parts of the museum, old photos, artifacts, storyboards and videos illustrate in great detail the three years Singapore was occupied by the Japanese.

The factory years

The former factory, built with an investment of US$735,425, boasted a state-of-the-art assembly that could turn out 40 vehicles a day with a workforce of some 400 men. It was not Ford's first venture into vehicle assembly in Singapore; this was contracted to the locally-based dealership, Wearnes Brothers, which assembled Ford vehicles in their workshop on Orchard Road at a rate of 18 cars a day. The factory, which was seized by the Japanese and made its military headquarters two days before the fall, recommenced assembly work in 1947. It continued operations until June 1980 when it was sold to neighboring Hume Industries. The area, formerly an industrial zone, was rezoned for residential use in the mid-1990s. The building lost a rear portion before it was made a National Monument in 2006 – the same year the Memories at Old Ford Factory opened in it as a permanent exhibition. This exhibition was revamped in 2017 and has been renamed Syonan Years: Singapore Under Japanese Rule (1942–1945).

LITTLE GUILIN

A rare survivor of Singapore's former natural hillocks

Bukit Batok Town Park
Bukit Batok East Ave 5
MRT: Bukit Gombak

Singapore is a pretty flat place. Most of the natural hillocks it once had have been flattened over the decades and pushed to the edges of the country to extend the shoreline. Since the government started its land reclamation push about a half century ago, Singapore is about a quarter larger and mostly bereft of its original ridges, cliffs and dramatic rock formations (see page 22).

With a few exceptions.

In the 104-acre Bukit Batok Town Park in northwestern Singapore, a serene lake is framed by some pretty burly rocks. Called "Little Guilin" because of its resemblance to a similarly scenic place in Guilin, China, the tranquil lake is actually a flooded quarry, the former Gammon Quarry on the slopes of Bukit Gombak. Mining of granite, and similar norite and gabbro rocks, started in the 19th century, as they were essential ingredients in the production of concrete. Between the 1950s and 1970s the quarrying business was booming thanks to Singapore's frenzied post-war building craze and the creation of Housing Development Board flats.

In Malay, *bukit* means "hill" and *batok* means "coughing", a name that stuck to the area because of the blasting noises that once came from the busy quarries. Several dotted the hilly areas around the Bukit Timah Nature Reserve – Bukit Batok, Bukit Gombak, Bukit Panjang – including the Singapore, Dairy Farm and Hindehede quarries. At 133 meters tall, Bukit Gombak is Singapore's second highest hill after Bukit Timah (see page 166). It's believed to be a part of Singapore's oldest rock formations dating back more than 250 million years to the Paleozoic age.

As the population and development of Singapore grew, operating quarries were approaching their maximum depths and also became problematic due to safety concerns from the blasting, both to humans and the environment. Singapore looked to neighboring countries for the rock chips it needed, and by the 1980s and 90s, all of the quarries dotting northwestern Singapore were abandoned. Some were filled in and paved over with roads and covered by apartment towers, while others collected rainwater and were swallowed up by the jungle and hidden from view or tidied up and incorporated into parks, like Lake Guilin.

NANTAH ARCH

The former entrance to the first Chinese language university outside China

Jurong West Street 93
MRT: Pioneer

Cut off from the road on which vehicles could once pass through it, the Nantah Arch looks out of place in an empty field at the edge of a residential neighborhood. The purpose of the arch on Jurong West Street 93 can be found on its centerpiece where the Chinese characters 南洋大學 (*Nanyang daxu*) appear.

Chinese for Nanyang University, Nanda or Nantah in short, *Nanyang* ("southern ocean") is a term used by the Chinese diaspora to refer to Southeast Asia or to Malaya and Singapore.

Although there seems little hint of the university in the area that surrounds it, Nantah Arch was once the main entrance to the first Chinese language university outside China, one built through the community's efforts.

The institution was the brainchild of rubber magnate and community leader Tan Lark Sye, who set it up in 1950 in response to the exclusion of a Chinese faculty at the University of Malaya. Tan donated $5 million and persuaded much of the community to also contribute. A 500-acre site was donated by the Hokkien Huay Kuan clan association that Tan headed. Construction began in 1953 and in a matter of two years the university would be up and running.

Chinese language education would see a decline following Singapore's independence, leading to the demise of Nanyang University. It merged with the National University of Singapore (NUS) in 1980. In 1981, the NUS' Nanyang Technological Institute was established at the campus. This became Nanyang Techological University in 1991. Although the arch and the former administration building still exist and the Nanyang name is being kept alive, the school that once sprawled there and the legacy of founder Tan Lark Sye have all but been forgotten.

The symbolism of Nantah Arch

Distinctly Chinese, the design of the arch has much symbolism attached to it. Topped with a Chinese-style roof, it has three portals below. The three represent heaven, earth and humankind, a trio that Chinese philosophy believes must be in a complementary relationship for the universe to exist.

The sections further symbolize gateways to three "talents," the acquisition of which is the goal of traditional Chinese education. The "talents" are *da cai*, the wisdom to govern; *chang cai*, capabilities of a trade; and *qing cai*, the ethics of man.

GARDEN OF FAME

From Goh's Folly to Goh's Glory

Jurong Hill Park
1 Jurong Hill
MRT: Boon Lay with a connection via Bus No. 194

Green and leafy Jurong Hill Park in the west of Singapore sits smack in the middle of an otherwise gray industrial and port area known for its shipyards, oil refineries and chemicals factories. Inside the park is

the forgotten Garden of Fame, a place where visiting foreign dignitaries started coming in the late 1960s to plant trees and get their name on a plaque. It was both a photo op and a clever way for Singapore to show foreign heads of state Jurong's budding industrial prowess.

Some 30 trees were planted over more than a decade before they ran out of space: the first was planted in 1969 by Princess Alexandra of the United Kingdom, and the last in 1984 by Dr. Albert Winsemius, an economic advisor to Singapore and a pioneer of industrialization. Other notable tree planters included Chinese Vice Premier Deng Xiaoping, Canadian Prime Minister Pierre Elliot Trudeau, Indonesia President Suharto, England's Queen Elizabeth II, American Vice President Spiro Agnew, Crown Prince Harald of Norway, Japanese Crown Prince Akihito and President of Singapore Benjamin Sheares.

It was once a tract of swamps, mangroves and jungle, a backwater where pepper, gambier and nutmeg plantations cropped up in the 19th century, replaced later by rubber, chives, and fish and prawn farms, and then brick works with their towering chimneys. But by the early 1960s, change was afoot in western Singapore. Hills were leveled and the shoreline was expanded and islands connected through land reclamation, priming the Jurong area to become a major commercial port and industrial hub at the urging of Singapore's Minister of Finance, Dr. Goh Keng Swee. Singapore couldn't keep relying on stagnating industries like banking and insurance (though today, private banking is an economic linchpin) and had no choice but to diversify its economy to create more jobs. At the time his detractors called the industrialization push "Goh's Folly." Later, after its success, it became "Goh's Glory."

To bestow some green on the industrial scene as more people moved to Jurong to be close to their jobs in all those new factories, Jurong Hill, also known by its Malay name Bukit Peropok, was officially made into a park in 1968. A seven-story look-out tower was built to offer views of western Singapore, the ship-choked sea and all those famous trees.

In keeping with the Garden City movement of that era, Jurong Bird Park opened nearby in 1971, followed by Japanese Gardens in 1973 and, two years later, the Chinese Gardens, keeping Singapore's first industrial region green with envy.

MACHINE-GUN PILLBOX

Historic defense post

Pasir Panjang
corner of Pasir Panjang and Science Park roads
MRT: Haw Par Villa

Passers-by are forgiven for overlooking this nondescript mound of weathered concrete. Hunkered along the roadside near the corner of Pasir Panjang and Science Park roads, in an area better known for high-tech industrial parks, this squat and boxy structure looks more like random urban infrastructure than the World War II relic that it is.

Pillboxes such as this were erected in the 1930s along Singapore's eastern and southern coasts to defend the island against sea invasion. At the time, they would likely have been hidden from view, either partially buried or concealed by dense vegetation. From inside the cramped hot enclosures, machine gunners could fire through openings, called loopholes, which are located on the front and in the small dome top of this particular pillbox. Pillboxes in Singapore came in many shapes and sizes and were strategically situated at intervals so that the gunfire would provide an overlapping sweep of coverage against invaders.

A handful of these defense posts can be found around Singapore. During WWII, the pillbox (see photo opposite), was manned by the 1st Malaya Brigade in its fierce defense of the Pasir Panjang Ridge against the advancing Japanese 18th Division. Today, anyone can view it from the outside but the entrance is locked.

Another pillbox is found in a sandy patch at the edge of Labrador Park, near the entrance to Keppel Harbour. The site of this machine gun bunker was known in the 19th century as Fort Pasir Panjang, one of nearly a dozen coastal artillery forts built by the British to defend Singapore.

Pillboxes

These miniature concrete fortresses were named for their shape, similar to the tiny boxes used for carrying medicines during the turn of the last century. Pillboxes first came into use in Europe during the First World War, and in the Second World War were erected across Great Britain to defend against a German sea attack that fortunately never happened. In Singapore, the British built a series of them as part of their beach defenses, protecting key military installations in the south that included ammunition depots and the Alexandra Military Hospital.

THE ORIGINAL STEPS TO HAW PAR VILLA

A Hell of a Park

262 Pasir Panjang Rd.
6872–2003
Daily 9am–7pm
Free
MRT: Haw Par Villa

Two tiers of entrance stairs are all that remains of a once grand circular-shaped villa designed by the famous local architect Ho Kwong Yew (who designed a similar house that still stands off Grange Road) for the wealthy Aw brothers in the late 1930s. It was damaged during WWII and then torn down shortly after.

The villa was the jewel in the crown of the Tiger Balm Gardens (also known as Haw Par Villa), a morality "garden" that was built in Singapore in 1937 by Aw Boon Haw (1882–1954) for his younger brother Aw Boon Par (1888–1944). The eccentric pair found their fortune making Tiger Balm ointment for sore muscles. They spent nearly US$2 million to build their dream park and the stunning villa on top of a hill along Pasir Panjang Road with panoramic views of the sea. When the Japanese occupied Singapore and took over the property during WWII, they used the house as a watchtower to keep a lookout for enemy ships.

Filled with more than 1,000 statues and 150 life-size dioramas illustrating Chinese folklore, fables and traditional values, the park is a wonderland of classic battles between good and evil, played out in colorful, flamboyant and sometimes horror-movie imagery. There are bloody faces, limbless bodies and creepy combinations of man and beast. The Ten Courts of Hell diorama shows in gory detail the agonizing tortures that await the damned for every sin committed. On the other end of the spectrum: a filial woman nurses her mother-in-law while her own infant waits his turn.

Though English-educated, the brothers cherished their Chinese heritage and wanted to create a public garden where families could immerse themselves in Chinese culture free of charge, while at the same time promoting their little jars of pain relief. Through various renovations and re-incarnations the hearty dioramas survived all these years.

Today, kitschy hexagonal jars of Tiger Balm are sold in more than 100 countries. It all started with Chinese herbalist Aw Chu Kin in Rangoon, Burma in the 1870s. On his deathbed, he beseeched his sons, Boon Haw and Boon Par, to continue making his medicinal ointment. The brothers turned the humble cure-all into a huge success before migrating to Singapore in the 1920s and opening a factory in Tanjong Pagar. The stuff was produced in the still-standing Eng Aun Tong factory at 89 Neil Road until 1971. It's now made in Jurong.

THE GAP

Location of Singapore's first street motor-races

Intersection of Kent Ridge Road and South Buona Vista Road
MRT: Kent Ridge

← MARINA HILL

PRINCE EDWARD POINT →

BY GRACIOUS CONSENT OF
HER MAJESTY QUEEN ELIZABETH II
THIS RIDGE WAS NAMED
KENT RIDGE
BY
THE GOVERNOR OF SINGAPORE H.E. SIR JOHN NICOLL K C M G
IN PART PLAY BY
H R H The DUCHESS OF KENT
AND
H R H The DUKE OF KENT
ON 5 OCTOBER 1952

Few memories remain of the Gap Hill Climb, a motorcycle race first run in 1927 – that later involved motorcars – and ended in 1973. The venue, as described by the race name, The Gap, is a saddle at the west end of a 5½-mile-long ridge line running parallel to Singapore's south-western coast. The gap permitted the construction of a road (South Buona Vista Road) across the ridge. It is known today for its sharp turns that are quite uncommon on Singapore roads: few know its racing history and just how challenging those bends in the road had been.

The name "The Gap" (synonymous also with the scenic views it presented of the coast) also has faded into obscurity and all that identifies its location is a marker that does not even mention its name. What the marker provides is the origins of the name "Kent Ridge" – the plaque encased in concrete was put up to commemorate the 1952 visit to the area's army units by the Duchess of Kent, Princess Marina, and her son, the Duke of Kent, Prince Edward.

The marker also speaks of The Gap's and Kent Ridge's military past. The army units were in place due to the strategic value of the ridge's elevated position overlooking the coast on which military installations and observation positions were established. Heavily defended during the Japanese invasion during World War II, the ridge witnessed one of the fiercest battles fought in the final days before Singapore fell.

The first Gap Hill Climb races were organized by the Singapore Volunteer Corps. Three were held on an annual basis for the benefit of the Corp's motorcycle platoon. It was discontinued after 1929 and it wasn't until 1939 that the Automobile Association of Malaya revived the races. The races were disrupted by the war and run again from 1948 through 1973 by the Singapore Motor Sports Club. More than three decades later, the Formula 1 night street racing circuit came to Singapore in 2007 for a now-yearly weekend race. Few people realize Singapore's motor-racing history had started much earlier.

The ridge west of The Gap has since 1976 been the home of the National University of Singapore, Singapore's first university. Besides Kent Ridge being named after the Duchess and Duke, it also can be surmised that the Duchess and the Duke had lent their names to Marina Hill, just east of The Gap, and Prince Edward Point, to its west.

YING FO FUI KUN CEMETERY

⑭

Singapore's last Hakka cemetery

9 Commonwealth Lane, Singapore 149551
Daily 8am–6:30pm
MRT: Commonwealth

Bounded by blocks of public housing flats and train tracks, the surprising Ying Fo Fui Kun cemetery contains some 2,700 tombstones laid out in 65 neat rows. Regularly rectangular, each stone is of the same shape and size, and they are all engraved with the same year – 1969, the year these bodies were exhumed and cremated.

Also known as Shuang Long Shan ('Double Dragon Hill') cemetery, it gets its name from two hills in the middle of the cemetery when it was established in 1887.

The cemetery remembers Hakkas, one of the five main Chinese groups in Singapore (the others being Hokkien, Teochew, Cantonese and Hainanese). It is the last Hakka cemetery in Singapore today.

Ying Fo Fui Kun, which manages the cemetery, is a Hakka clan association founded in 1822. Its name reflects the founders' aspirations of mutual support and peaceful co-existence among Hakkas in Singapore. As in the earlier days of Singapore's history, Hakka people came from five different counties in Canton, China. The clan used to own about 100 acres of land in this area.

In 1966, much of the land was acquired for residential use, under the Housing Development Board. The land was flattened, and the remains were exhumed and cremated, with the ashes in urns either under the headstones or kept in ancestral halls.

The uniform headstones here were designed and put up by the Board. The front row consists of 12 larger, stepped headstones that stand out from the rest; these most probably belonged to those with richer families.

The 4.5-acre plot of land also houses an ancestral hall.

THE PLAQUE OF ALEXANDRA HOSPITAL

WWII horrors that took place at a hospital

Alexandra Hospital
378 Alexandra Road
MRT: Queenstown, then Bus #51 or #195

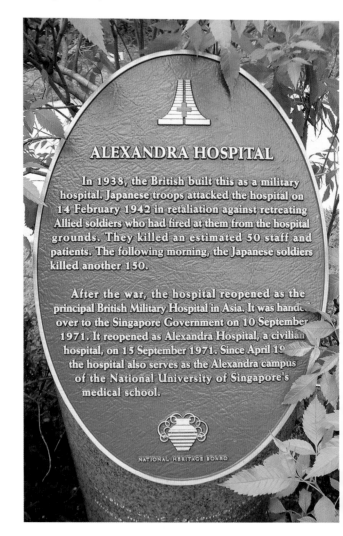

ALEXANDRA HOSPITAL

In 1938, the British built this as a military hospital. Japanese troops attacked the hospital on 14 February 1942 in retaliation against retreating Allied soldiers who had fired at them from the hospital grounds. They killed an estimated 50 staff and patients. The following morning, the Japanese soldiers killed another 150.

After the war, the hospital reopened as the principal British Military Hospital in Asia. It was handed over to the Singapore Government on 10 September 1971. It reopened as Alexandra Hospital, a civilian hospital, on 15 September 1971. Since April 19 the hospital also serves as the Alexandra campus of the National University of Singapore's medical school.

NATIONAL HERITAGE BOARD

In front of Alexandra Hospital's main entrance, it is easy to miss a small plaque nestled in the lush, peaceful park. The text reveals the savagery that happened here in WWII.

Japanese troops, having overtaken Malaya, crossed the Strait of Johor and within days had advanced to the south of the island. The morning of February 14, 1942 they descended upon the British Military Hospital, as Alexandra Hospital was formerly known, shelling it heavily. The hospital already was packed to almost double capacity, water was rationed and light was only allowed for medical procedures. At around 1pm, a lone Japanese soldier was spotted advancing toward the hospital. A British military captain from the 32nd Company of the Royal Army Medical Corps ventured out to meet him, pointing to his Red Cross armband to alert him to the hospital's presence. Despite the gesture, the Japanese soldier opened fire on the captain, just missing him. The captain ran back inside the hospital but by then three enemy platoons had surrounded the compound.

That afternoon, Japanese soldiers raided the hospital, storming every room, where they shot, bayoneted and beat doctors, hospital staff and patients. Not even an anesthetized patient on the operating table was spared. About 50 men were killed while 200 others, including the gravely injured, were bound in groups of eight and forcibly marched to a nearby row of outhouses. Injured prisoners who fell were killed. The prisoners spent the night packed into three small rooms, where some died overnight. The survivors left the rooms the following morning, lead two-by-two by Japanese soldiers who promised them water but executed them instead. It was only after Japanese forces resumed fighting that morning that a shell hit the building where the prisoners were kept, allowing some to escape before being summarily executed.

The British Military Hospital was built during the late 1930s as the principal hospital for Britain's Far East Command during World War II. It was converted to a civilian hospital in 1971 and renamed Alexandra Hospital. In 1992, a team from the hospital and Ministry of Defense explored a mysterious network of brick-lined tunnels built under the hospital (the red-brick entrance to the tunnel can be spotted just to the right of the main hospital entrance.) They discovered medicine jars and bottles from the pre-war period, leading them to conclude that the tunnels were constructed when the hospital was built. Might they have been used by survivors who escaped the massacre?

FORMER BREWMASTER'S HOUSE ⑯

*All that remains today of the once thriving factory
complex where Anchor Beer was produced*

Anchorpoint Shopping Centre
370 Alexandra Road
MRT: Queenstown

An important and certainly coveted post, a brewmaster's job is to taste his factory's beer and give it his stamp of approval before it's shipped off to thirsty customers. For the Archipelago Brewery Company (ABC), its top taster had the added privilege of occupying the two-story brewmaster's house along Alexandra Road, near the junction with Queensway. Repurposed as a restaurant in recent years, the white building with a red peaked roof is all that remains today of the once thriving factory complex where Anchor beer was produced. The beer, however, lives on in its name at the site; behind the brewmaster's former house is the Anchorpoint Shopping Centre and behind it, The Anchorage condo, both launched in 1997.

Owned by German businessmen and opened in 1933 on the location of a former rubber plantation, the multi-million dollar brewery's main product was Anchor Beer, a light pilsner made with English hops and Australian malt. Just down the road was a competitor, Malayan Breweries (MBL), that a year earlier started producing Tiger Beer, a pale lager and Singapore's first locally brewed beer. Today it's considered by most to be Singapore's national beer.

Alexandra Road was a popular site for factories back in the early decades of the 20th century; it was close to the Malayan Railway line and thus convenient for transporting the goods. Brewing was done in the main plant where the Anchorpoint mall now stands. The bottled beer was transported via a wooden conveyor belt across an overhead bridge to the canning line, where the yellow and blue IKEA store now resides.

In 1939, with World War II looming, Singapore's British colonial government claimed the ABC brewery as enemy property and sold it two years later to MBL, a joint venture between local soft drinks producer, Fraser & Neave (F&N), and Dutch brewer, Heineken. Production of both Anchor and Tiger beers continues to this day, though in 1990 operations moved to Tuas and the name was changed to Asia Pacific Breweries, which after a 2013 merger, became Heineken Asia Pacific.

FULLERTON HOTEL LIGHTHOUSE BEACON  ⑰

A much lower point than it was originally intended

Mapletree Business City
Near 20 Pasir Panjang Rd
MRT: Pasir Panjang

Occupying a much lower point than was originally intended, a lighthouse beacon sits on a little grassy patch at the entrance of Mapletree Business City, its second home since it was decommissioned in 1979. Before that, the beacon was down the road atop the Fullerton Building, once part of a lighthouse there. Its revolving beacon had guided ships to the safety of the harbor below.

Singapore's main lighthouse originally sat atop Fort Canning Hill, which was at one time close to the shore and clearly visible to ships out at sea. In 1855, ships were guided into the harbor and up the Singapore River by a lone lantern hung from a flagstaff at the top of the hill. In 1902, Fort Canning Hill got a proper lighthouse. At 80 feet tall atop the 119 foot hill, it reached a total elevation of 199 feet and was visible for more than 18 ½ miles.

As land reclamation pushed the shoreline outward and nearby high rises blocked the view, the Fort Canning lighthouse was rendered useless. The Fullerton Building, built in 1928, was chosen as the new location for a new lighthouse – the Fullerton Lighthouse was commissioned in 1958.

Named after the first governor of the Straits Settlements, Robert Fullerton, the massive Fullerton Building housed government offices, the best known of which was the General Post Office. It had replaced Fort Fullerton, which sat at the water's edge protecting the mouth of the Singapore River – a perfect location for a signal. A 540-kilocandelas, electric-powered beacon was installed, which was visible for 18 miles.

For over two decades the beacon guided the cargo ships as they navigated the busy waters of the harbor and bumboats as they plied their way between ships and go-downs, or warehouses, alongside the river. By the late 1970s, it was again dwarfed by high-rises and that's why it was eventually retired and moved to its current location. Meanwhile, a restaurant atop The Fullerton Hotel, called The Lighthouse Restaurant & Rooftop Bar, commands one of the finest views in town.

WHITE OBELISK AT LABRADOR PARK

Located here to be noticed as a navigation aid

Navigation Marker
Labrador Park
MRT: Labrador Park

In southwest Singapore, where Labrador Park fronts the sea, a verdant and rocky promontory contains several military structures, including the remnants of a 19th-century coastal artillery pillbox (see page 176), one of the last of its kind in Singapore. The promontory is known as Tanjong Berlayer, which is Malay for "Sailing Cape" – a hint of its nautical significance.

Not far from the pillbox, at the south end of the park, a strange white pillar-like structure stands, serving seemingly no apparent purpose. Or does it? While it is presently hidden in shadows, the white obelisk was originally located here to be noticed as a navigation aid. White obelisks such as this were once placed along coastal areas as fixed navigation reference points or markers.

However, this particular obelisk replaced a centuries-old navigation reference point – a rock known as Batu Berlayer, which was removed in 1848 to widen the entrance to Keppel Harbor. The rock was identified as far back as the 16th century, but it may actually have been known earlier. In his travelogue *Daoyi Zhilüe*, 14th-century Chinese traveler Wang Dayuan described an entrance to a harbor in the area that he called Long Yamen or "Dragon-Teeth Gate," which is also shown in records linked to Admiral Zheng He's 15th-century voyages. It has been suggested that this ancient harbor entrance was Batu Berlayer, with the other "tooth" at Tanjong Rimau across the channel on Sentosa. Batu Berlayer, known to the British as "Lot's Wife," also appears in accounts of both Portuguese and Dutch voyagers to the region from the 16th and 17th centuries, including Dutchman Jan Huyghen van Linschoten's account of his late 16th-century voyage to the East Indies, *Itinerario*.

The obelisk that replaced Batu Berlayer marked the western extremity of Singapore's harbor. A corresponding white obelisk was used to mark the harbor's eastern end at Siglap. The obelisk itself was replaced by the red and very noticeable Berlayer Beacon just after World War II.

A replica of Batu Berlayer rock was erected close to its original spot in 2005 to commemorate the 600th Anniversary of Admiral Zheng He's voyages to the region.

A WARTIME JAPANESE GRAVE ⑲

A grave for the adventurous

Mount Faber (near Wishart Road)
MRT: Telok Blangah

After a 10- to 15-minute walk uphill through thick vegetation from the forest's edge at Mount Faber's Wishart Road, the reward is coming face-to-face with a 6½ foot pillar-like structure supported on a three-tiered base of concrete. It's quite clearly the headstone of a Japanese grave even with its larger than usual proportions.

Japanese inscriptions marked on the face of the headstone reveal the identity of the person buried in the grave as Omoto Egasa (小本江笠). Inscriptions in Chinese script found on the headstone's other faces provide further information on Omoto. A naval architect, Omoto was an employee of Mitsubishi Heavy industries' Kobe Shipyard who brought over the first batch of Japanese shipyard workers on March 2, 1942 – just two weeks after the fall of Singapore. Having contracted an illness while working tirelessly on a shipbuilding project, Omoto perished on July 18, 1942 at the age of 47, just three months after he had arrived.

However, nothing explains the nature of Omoto's illness or the choice of the grave's isolated location. Perhaps, its perch allowed Omoto to watch over the works his men were carrying out in the Singapore Harbour Board's dry docks below.

For the adventurous, the slopes of Mount Faber present numerous opportunities for discovery. The hill has a long association with the military, which coveted the elevation for its strategic perch over the harbor, leaving behind a network of shafts and tunnels and military posts. Its southern slope is particularly intriguing with several colonial houses built as homes for the senior members of the Singapore Harbour Board and the ancestral cemetery of the current Sultans of Johor.

The freshwater red brick-lined reservoir there possibly dates to the late 19th century. More recently it appears to have been used as a recreational bathing spot with the remnants of a diving platform clearly visible. Parts of a filtration system for the supply of fresh water are also in evidence. The reservoir is a useful landmark in locating the mysterious lone Japanese grave some 300 feet away, further up the slope, via a well-worn flight of red brick steps to the east.

HARBOURFRONT 19TH-CENTURY STEAM CRANE ㉒

A crane designed to run on a railroad track remains even though railroad tracks do not

55 Pasir Panjang Road
SCC@Harbourfront
MRT: HarbourFront

Agenuine curiosity, the old crane languishing in the weeds beside the Singapore Cruise Centre at Harbourfront, just off Pasir Panjang Road, is a wink to this area's heritage as one of Singapore's most important ports.

In technical terms, a locomotive crane is designed to run on a railroad track to move freight on and off boats. This one was made in 1879 by John H. Wilson & Co. of Liverpool, England. It was powered by a steam engine, had a capacity of 10 tons, and ran on 7' gauge rail tracks. Its vertical boiler was made by Walter W. Coltman & Co., Central Boiler Works, Loughborough, UK. The crane was made for the privately-owned Tanjong Pagar Dock Company. As far back as the 1830s, the Tanjong Pagar area had been occupied by a vast nutmeg plantation, but with the advent of steamships in the 1860s, followed by the 1869 opening of the Suez Canal, spice cultivation was uprooted for more lucrative endeavors in shipping. The Tanjong Pagar Dock Company built Victoria Dock in 1868, and with rising demand for ship repair, it opened another dock, Albert Dock, in 1879. It was for the latter dock that this crane was made to move goods between ships in ports and rail cars.

As shipping became a major driver of economic prosperity for Singapore, the "New Harbour" in Tanjong Pagar (later named Keppel Harbour) was abuzz with goods transferred between here and the Singapore River godowns, or warehouses. However, the Tanjong Pagar Dock Company was perhaps a bit too successful, controlling almost all the land in the region that was capable of wharfing large ocean-going steam vessels. As a result, the government of the Straits Settlements took over the company in 1905 and formed the Tanjong Pagar Dock Board. In 1983 the Port Authority of Singapore (PSA) filled in both Albert Dock and Victoria Dock to expand the nearby container terminal. Surprisingly, this little steamy was in operation until the very end, serving over an entire century.

FORT IMBIAH BATTERY

A glimpse into Singapore's WWII military infrastructure for the more intrepid

Sentosa
Accessible from Imbiah Walk or Siloso Road, Sentosa, 24 hours
Occasional tours offered by organizations like the Singapore Heritage Board and My Community
MRT: Harbour Front, then hop on monorail or cable to Sentosa

I t is amazing that with all the glitzy tourist development of Sentosa Island, the remains of the Mount Imbiah Battery are still here in the overgrowth. According to the Sentosa Development Corporation, the underground passages of the Battery have become inhabited by a colony of around 100 edible-nest and black nest swiftlets, Singapore's largest flock of these bird species. The birds, which use echolocation to navigate in darkness, make nests from their saliva that are a prized delicacy for the Chinese. To protect the birds and their nests, the interior of the Mount Imbiah bunker is closed off to the public except for occasional tours offered by organizations like the Singapore Heritage Board and My Community, when you can walk through the old munitions storage facilities that have literally "gone to the birds."

Pulau Blakang Mati: once a bastion of military might

Once upon a time, it was believed that Pulau Blakang Mati, now named Sentosa Island, would be the military savior of Singapore. The British colonial defenses built up the southern island with military infrastructure. Tourists are familiar with Fort Siloso, but the lesser-known Mount Imbiah Battery is lost to thick tropic jungle. It was built as a redoubt to support the other forts, and today provides a glimpse into Singapore's WWII military infrastructure for the more intrepid curiosity hunter.

Pulau Blakang Mati was part of Singapore's defense strategy as early as 1827. In the 1880s, three artillery forts, Serapong, Connaught and Siloso, were erected along with the Mount Imbiah Battery. Siloso and Imbiah were positioned to defend the Western entrance to Singapore harbor. Imbiah was built to hold 82 infantry soldiers and 19 gunners. In 1914 at the start of World War I, one of the most powerful coastal defense guns at the time, a 9.2 inch coastal gun, was emplaced there.

In the mid-1930s Mount Imbiah Battery was deserted for Fort Connaught, in the southeast of Blakang Mati, which also received Imbiah's coastal guns. However, Imbiah was still manned and used as a reserve magazine for storing ammunition until the fall of Singapore to the Japanese in 1942.

SENTOSA BOARDWALK

Sections of old monorail line survive in the jungles of Sentosa

Sentosa Island
MRT: HarbourFront to Sentosa Express monorail

Venture by foot or bicycle along Sentosa's Imbiah Walk, hang a left on the Imbiah Trail just before the Costa Sands Hotel and then look up. Above you are some rusty old sections of monorail track that are abruptly chopped off – like part of an aging set on an abandoned stage.

The 1 1/4-mile-long Imbiah Trail dates back to Sentosa's early days in the 1970s. Few trekkers or cyclists realize that a newer segment of the walk – a length of boardwalk that skims over the top of thick foliage – actually was converted from old monorail tracks that once snaked through the island.

Before the shiny bullet-shaped Sentosa Express train opened in 2007, visitors to Sentosa explored the island aboard the Sentosa Monorail. Slow and easy, the open-air train rambled between attractions along a raised rail that meandered over hills and through forests offering some pretty natural vistas. Thankfully, some of the most picturesque portions of the old monorail have been transformed into a boardwalk.

The Sentosa Nature Discovery Centre also was converted from an old monorail station. The center's unique displays provide a scientific framework for the natural scenery along the trail, preparing visitors for an "edutaining" nature walk along Imbiah Trail.

The trail winds around 37 acres of forest on Mount Imbiah and is chock full of wildlife. Trekkers are treated to three manmade waterfalls along the way to the summit of Mount Imbiah, 197 feet above sea level, where they will find the remnants of the World War II Ft. Imbiah Battery (which is now inhabited by Singapore's only remaining swiftlet colony, see previous double-page spread). There's also a 33-foot-high bird-watching tower with scenic views of Singapore's Southern Islands.

The Imbiah Nature Walk is just one part of six walking trails on Sentosa – about 4 2/3 miles of trekking – that connect to the Southern Ridges trail system. The "Sentosa Walking Trails" include the new Sentosa Boardwalk, Southeast Asia's only garden-themed boardwalk. Connecting Sentosa to the mainland, the more than one-third-mile boardwalk is landscaped with exhibits of five habitats that can be found on Sentosa: mangrove, rock garden, terrain and hill, coastal flora, and secondary rainforest.

THE TOWERS OF LIGHTS SEEN FROM GHOST ISLAND

A wonderful escape from the urban world

Pulau Hantu (Ghost Island)
Chartered boat from West Coast Pier, 60 West Coast Ferry Road

For those brave enough to visit an isolated place with a sinister name, Pulau Hantu, or "Ghost Island," provides a wonderful escape from the urban world. Located several miles off the southwestern coast of Singapore, it has long been a destination for camping and picnics for those with the means to charter a boat to get there. An overnight camping trip – possible with a permit from the Singapore Land Authority – brings out a side of the island that few people know about: the sight of magical towers of light emanating from nearby Pulau Bukom Besar.

Pulau Bukom Besar was the first of Singapore's islands to be industrialized – as quite a few in the southwest have. Shell, which operates a refinery and petrochemical processing complex there, was first associated with it in 1891. That was when the company purchased the island for kerosene storage. The company established Singapore's first refinery on the island in 1961. Since then, Bukom has been joined to two of its neighboring islands, Pulau Busing and Pulau Ular to its west. The expanded petrochemical complex developed on the enlarged land mass. At night it's quite an amazing sight when the lights of the industrial stacks are lit and reflect off the water.

Pulau Hantu is actually made up of two islets, Pulau Hantu Besar ("Greater Ghost Island") and Pulau Hantu Kecil ("Lesser Ghost Island"), connected across a tidal flat visible at low tide. The flat is said to vanish, like a ghost, with the rising tide and this offers one explanation of the island's rather curious name. With land reclamation in the 1970s, Pulau Hantu was expanded and swimming lagoons lined by palm-fringed beaches became a part of the topography. Reefs surrounding the island also draw divers and fishermen. Visibility can be quite poor, between about 1 and 3 meters, though from time to time there are good days when divers can see colorful tropical fish and interesting little sea creatures. At one point there were plans to turn Pulau Hantu into a holiday destination, but nothing came of it and now the island serves as an escape for the few who know about it.

There is no regular boat service to the island, but it is possible to make the half-hour journey there with a boat chartered from West Coast Pier. Besides a camping permit, some food, drinking water, mosquito repellent and camping gear is recommended for an overnight stay. Comfort facilities are available on the island.

RAFFLES LIGHTHOUSE

Named after the founder of modern Singapore

Pulau Satumu
www.mpa.gov.sg/web/portal/home/maritime-singapore/public-outreach/mpalj
Access possible through "Learning Journeys"

Singapore comprises more than 50 islands, though just a few are widely known. Standing on Singapore's southernmost island, Pulau Satumu or Coney Islet, Raffles Lighthouse is just about as far south as you can get in Singapore's tiny universe (not to be confused with a beacon at Raffles Marina in Tuas commonly referred to as "Raffles Marina Lighthouse"). One of only five operated by Singapore's Maritime and Port Authority (MPA), the Raffles Lighthouse looks over the western entrance to the congested waters of the Straits of Singapore. The MPA offers Learning Journeys tours from time to time, including a visit to the Raffles Lighthouse (see their website opposite).

The lighthouse is one of only two to which lighthouse keepers, a rare breed these days, are sent. Teams of two keepers are rotated every 10 days. Each keeper works a 12-hour shift during which rounds are made and equipment, including the beacon at the top of the 72-foot-high lighthouse, is maintained. Getting to the top is a workout that involves climbing 107 steps. The beacon, once fired by kerosene and, since 1968, a convert to electricity, is now a powerful combination of halogen lamps and metal reflectors and is visible 20 nautical miles away.

Named after the founder of modern Singapore, Sir Stamford Raffles, the foundation stone for the lighthouse was laid on May 24, 1854 – the birthday of Queen Victoria – to much ceremony. With the help of convict labor and with building materials obtained from the granite island of Pulau Ubin in Singapore's north, Raffles Lighthouse would be completed 1½ years later – Singapore's second lighthouse. The first, Horsburgh Lighthouse, was built at the eastern entrance of the Singapore Strait just four years earlier in 1851.

Besides Raffles and Horsburgh, the MPA also operates offshore lighthouses at Sultan Shoal and Pulau Pisang. The latter, which is in Malaysian territory, is the second lighthouse that requires keepers. There is also one lighthouse onshore, Bedok Lighthouse, sitting in a very Singaporean fashion right on the top of a 25-story apartment block in Marine Parade.

A holiday apartment used by late Dr Goh Keng Swee

The lighthouse is typical in appearance as lighthouses of the era go. Hidden behind it, however, in much less typical fashion, is a holiday apartment appended to its base and used by members of the port authority's senior staff. The seclusion provided by the island was also just what the architect of Singapore's economic success, the late Dr Goh Keng Swee, sought in late 1959 when he locked himself in the apartment to work on his maiden budget speech as fully self-governing Singapore's first Finance Minister.

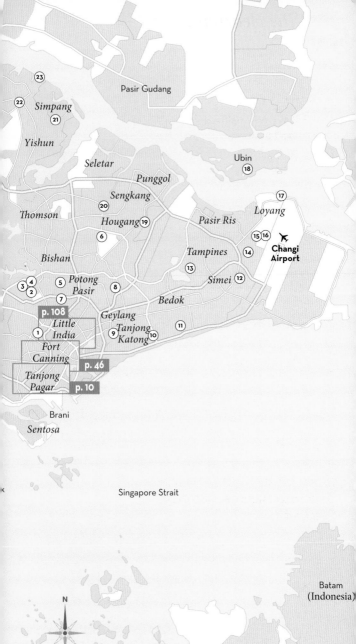

Pasir Gudang

㉓

㉒ *Simpang*

㉑

Yishun

Seletar

Punggol

Ubin
⑱

Thomson

Sengkang

⑳

Hougang ⑲

⑥

Loyang

⑰

Bishan

Potong Pasir
⑤

⑧

Pasir Ris

Tampines

⑬

⑮⑯

⑭

Changi
Airport

③④
②

⑦

Simei ⑫

Bedok

p. 108

Little India

Geylang

Tanjong Katong

⑨   ⑩

⑪

①

Fort Canning

p. 46

Tanjong Pagar

p. 10

Brani

Sentosa

Singapore Strait

Batam
(Indonesia)

N

0   5   10 km

The Heartland, East Coast and Changi

1. ONE-TWO-SIX CAIRNHILL ARTS CENTRE — 206
2. THE BLACK AND WHITE HOUSES AT MOUNT PLEASANT ROAD — 208
3. THE SIKH TOMB GUARDIANS OF BUKIT BROWN CEMETERY — 210
4. BUKIT BROWN PEACOCK TILES — 212
5. BLOCK 53 TOA PAYOH'S Y SHAPE — 214
6. JAPANESE CEMETERY PARK — 215
7. FIRST POSTWAR FILM STUDIO — 216
8. OLD KHONG GUAN BISCUIT FACTORY — 218
9. KALLANG AIRPORT RUNWAY — 220
10. OLD SEAWALLS & STEPS — 222
11. TOK LASAM'S GRAVE — 224
12. JACKIE CHAN'S ANCIENT CHINESE HOUSES — 226
13. RETRO TV TEST PATTERN MURALS — 228
14. OLD CHANGI PRISON GATES — 230
15. THE FACES OF CHANGI MURALS — 232
16. THE JOHORE BATTERY — 234
17. CHANGI BEACH MASSACRE MARKER — 236
18. TECK SENG'S PLACE — 238
19. STATUE OF THE BLESSED VIRGIN MARY — 240
20. KAMPONG LORONG BUANGKOK — 242
21. KAYAKING ON SUNGEI KHATIB BONGSU — 246
22. ADMIRALTY HOUSE BOMB SHELTER — 248
23. BEAULIEU HOUSE — 250

ONE-TWO-SIX CAIRNHILL ARTS CENTRE

Old Anglo-Chinese School

126 Cairnhill Road
MRT: Somerset

Built in 1925 on a little hill in the Orchard Road area, what is now One-Two-Six Cairnhill Arts Centre was designed by renowned colonial architect firm Swan & Maclaren, the people behind the Teutonia Club (now Goodwood Park Hotel) and Sultan Mosque, among other national treasures.

At the time of the building's construction as the Anglo-Chinese School (ACS), Swan & Maclaren led the way for modern architecture in Singapore. Now dwarfed among the towering giants around it, it's worth a good look: its "semi-Chinese style" as seen in details such as upturned eaves and geometrical motifs is a rare hybrid style nearly gone from the Singapore tableau.

At the time, the Cairnhill area was undergoing a construction boom in what was once a nutmeg plantation. In the mid-1800s, when Orchard Road was actually orchards, a man named Charles Carnie tended nearly 5,000 nutmeg trees atop "Carnie's Hill," thus the name, Cairn Hill. Over the years, shophouses and terrace houses were built along Cairnhill Road, with a few exceptional examples that have been preserved. Amid the circa 1920s row of houses in front of the school, numbers 128A-H were also designed by Swan & Maclaren.

Interesting, immediately following World War II, the campus was shared with Monk's Hill Primary School during a period when functional school buildings were in short supply.

After ACS moved out in 1949, the building continued to be occupied by educational institutions, including the National Institute for Education (NIE). Following preservation work in 1993, it reopened as an arts venue and is now known as One-Two-Six Cairnhill Arts Centre. While there are no immediate plans to redevelop the area, the government is studying the merits of conserving the building.

Old school

While virtually every Singaporean knows of the Anglo-Chinese School (ACS) at Barker Road, only a few oldtimers remember when the campus was at Cairnhill, tucked behind a row of Art Deco-style terrace houses. This address was one stop for the 125-year-old institution, which has become a symbol of educational excellence for Singapore's elite. However, despite its pedigree, the fate of the building is currently in limbo. ACS was founded in 1886 by Methodist Bishop William Fitzjames Oldham with 13 pupils in a small shophouse on Amoy Street. One year later, following a surge in enrollment, the school moved to larger premises at Coleman Street. By the 1920s, it had grown large enough to occupy this purpose-built facility, where it stayed for 24 years before landing its Barker Road home.

THE BLACK AND WHITE HOUSES AT MOUNT PLEASANT ROAD ②

Not as black and white as it seems

159 Mount Pleasant Road
Buses 54, 141, 162, 166, 167, 851 and 980 from MRT: Novena – Old Police
Academy Stop (51021)

Quiet and well shaded, Mount Pleasant Road seems everything its name hints. The road, lined with generously proportioned "black and white" residences, looks typical of one given to house Singapore's colonial administrators, except that the ample lawns of its houses hide the clues to an event that took place in the final moments of Singapore's darkest days.

One house that has given up some of its secrets is No. 159. Positioned near the top of the elevation that gives the road its name, No. 159 displays the distinctive features of the "black and white" or mock-Tudor style, a style most commonly employed by the Public Works Department in putting up the residences for the most senior of municipal officers between the 1920s and 1930s. Characteristics of the design include pitched roofs, wide verandahs and a large frontage of windows to maximize insulation and ventilation.

The grounds of No. 159 were where spent bullet cases fired in one of the last battles fought before Singapore's inglorious fall were uncovered. A long-buried cache of unused ammunition was also found, evidence of an unhurried surrender and an indication where the final line of battle had been drawn (photos of the excavated ammunition can be found on www.adamparkproject.com).

Further evidence, from interviews previously conducted with survivors of the battle on both sides, help complete the picture of a battle for which the events of February 14, 1942, provided a stage. It was the day before the fall that the invading Japanese force broke through Bukit Brown Municipal Cemetery, which lies across a valley on the northwest of Mount Pleasant. The desperate defenders, remnants of several British army units, retreated and took up positions in the houses along Mount Pleasant Road. One of the houses, No. 160 – just across the road from No. 159 – was captured during the night and this prompted an attempt to retake it on the morning of February 15, mounted from No. 159.

No. 160 was retaken with help from artillery positioned nearby. A dozen anti-tank rounds were blasted into the house, flushing the invaders out, but causing a fire. This outcome was to help in No. 160's identification as the house in question. Aerial photos some time after the war's end show 160 as the only house with a new roof, indicating it was newly rebuilt after the fire. While the battle may have been one of little consequence, it was significant in that it may have been one of the last, if not the last, successes on the British side. Just hours after the battle, on the afternoon of February 15, a ceasefire would be ordered not long after which Singapore fell to the Japanese victors.

THE SIKH TOMB GUARDIANS OF BUKIT BROWN CEMETERY

A crossing of cultures even in spaces given to the dead

Bukit Brown Cemetery, off Adam Road
Buses 74, 157 or 852 from MRT: Tan Kah Kee (Opp Tan Kah Kee Stn Stop 47019) to – Bef Sicc Stop (41141)

A huge Chinese burial site, Bukit Brown Cemetery is spread over some 400 acres of rolling landscape in central Singapore, its nearly 100,000 graves making it the largest Chinese cemetery outside of China. Amid the graves, several grave guardians present a break from the cemetery's Hokkien Chinese character. With their thick beards (except for a few) and turbans, at least 26 pairs of guardians – of humans in soldier-like garb – are unmistakably Sikh.

Sikhs are very much part of the multicultural and multi-religious social fabric of Singapore and it is perhaps no surprise that their statues have been used as tomb guardians. The first Sikhs to the region came over in the service of the British military or to work as policemen. Respected for their courage and sense of duty, many also found jobs in security services. It was common to see Sikh jagas – as security guards were referred to – standing guard at financial institutions and other establishments that would have included some owned by those buried in Bukit Brown.

Bukit Brown Cemetery opened as a municipal burial ground for the Hokkien Chinese in 1922. Closed to burials in 1973, the cemetery has grown wild with flora and fauna, prompting nature groups to call

for its preservation. Bukit Brown's value as a heritage site also has seen heritage groups adding their voices to the call. Unfortunately, their efforts have not changed the course of the cemetery's destiny as large parts of it will be redeveloped in the longer term for public housing. Parts of the cemetery already have been lost to roads. A realignment of Lornie Road in the 1960s took with it several hundred graves, and more recently, the construction of an 8-lane highway through Bukit Brown required the exhumation of 3,000 graves.

BUKIT BROWN PEACOCK TILES

Symbols of Beauty & Grace for the Departed

Bukit Brown Municipal Cemetery
MRT: Botanic Gardens

While decorative tiles are fairly common on tombs scattered around the sprawling nearly-century-old Bukit Brown Cemetery, those depicting peacocks are rare birds. Nestled in the foliage of the cemetery's block 2 are ornamental peacock tiles in single-, twin- and four-tile panels on a number of graves, including the Hokkien-Peranakan great-grandparents of Jennifer Lim, author of *Singapore Heritage Tiles: An International Mosaic of Love* (2021).

The twin tombs from 1936 are flanked by two peacock panels facing each other. Not too far away, in block 1, there are more peacock-themed tiles on the spectacular tomb of teenager Eddie Chan Sin Chuan, which was erected in the early days of the Japanese occupation of Singapore in the 1940s.

When Lim discovered Eddie Chan's tomb, it was nearly swallowed up by the jungle. Lim felt compelled to tidy it up out of respect, a temporary reprieve before the fast-growing foliage of Bukit Brown took back the tomb once again.

As decorative elements, peacocks, called kongquè (孔雀) in

Mandarin, can be seen on Chinese textiles as far back as 2,000 years, says Lim. In the Ming dynasty, peacocks adorned the clothing of high-ranking officers. Further status might also have been granted them due to their association with the phoenix, a mythical bird that represented supreme beauty and grace in Chinese culture, which would explain the bird's popularity on a site as sacred as a final resting place.

In Singapore's early days, peacock motif tiles like these would have been made in England, where an obsession with Eastern decorative elements was all the rage from the mid-18th century. In India, where the peacock is the national bird, it appears in many ancient artforms.

By the 1920s, however, peacock tiles would not have had to travel so far, as Japanese tile makers had entered the Southeast Asian and Indian markets with their own fine examples, supplying tiles for temples, tombs and lavish homes.

A Dutch Windmill on a Chinese Grave

Outside of the main gates of Bukit Brown cemetery, in the adjacent Seh Ong Hill cemetery, semi-circular tombs dot the grassy slopes along both sides of Kheam Hock Road. One grave from the 1960s features a series of six beautiful colorful tile panels, likely made in Japan, incorporating European and Asian landscapes. One tile panel reveals a Dutch windmill, one a European mountain scene, and another depicts a Japanese landscape with windswept pine trees, a fishing boat and Mt. Fuji.

The peaceful images are said to help surround the departed with the all-important elements of mountains and water for good feng shui, vital principles for many Chinese.

BLOCK 53 TOA PAYOH'S Y SHAPE ⑤

A one-of-a-kind shape for a VIP block

Toa Payoh Lorong 5
MRT: Braddell

With its rows of four two-bedroom flats along an airy common corridor, Block 53 in Toa Payoh looks just like any other public housing block built in the 1960s by the Housing and Development Board (HDB). But, because it was meant to have a special role as a "model estate" to be showcased to visiting dignitaries, it was designed in a unique Y-shaped plan, in order to stand out among the growing number of public housing complexes.

Built on a small elevation in the first satellite town over which the HDB had complete control in planning, Block 53 was the HDB's first purpose-built "VIP block."

Toa Payoh's tallest at its completion in 1967 with 19 floors, the block had a viewing deck on its roof to which dignitaries could be brought.

The new town, a symbol of the remarkable success Singapore had in

its public housing program, just had to be shown-off.

The first up the roof was John Gorton, prime minister of Australia, in April 1968. He would be followed by a string of prime ministers and heads of state. Royalty would grace the roof in February 1972, when Queen Elizabeth II, Prince Philip and Princess Anne visited. To complete the experience, dignitaries were also brought into one of the block's units.

The roof gallery has since been closed off. A new VIP block with a covered roof deck replaced Block 53 as a VIP Block in 1973.

JAPANESE CEMETERY PARK ⑥

The largest Japanese cemetery in Southeast Asia

Chuan Hoe Avenue
Daily 8am–6:30pm
MRT: Kovan

Few know that the largest and most well-preserved Japanese cemetery in Southeast Asia is in Singapore and that more than one-third of its 910 graves belong to karayuki-san, or Japanese prostitutes.

Occupying 30,000 square meters in Singapore's Serangoon North area, the Japanese Cemetery Park was founded in 1891 by three Japanese brothel keepers and rubber plantation owners. They obtained permission from the government to create a burial ground for *karayuki-san* who had worked in Singapore. The land for the resulting graveyard was carved partly from their own plantations. Besides the *karayuki-san*, over the decades, the cemetery would accommodate departed Japanese from all walks of life in keeping with the expanding Japanese expatriate community. Graves of the very wealthy were ornate, with stone sculptures of Jizo, a Japanese deity, or even Corinthian-style columns.

The cemetery contains memorials to World War II Japanese military casualties, including those who had committed suicide after the Japanese surrender and others who were executed as war criminals. In one corner, three memorial stones were placed by Japanese prisoners of war. Behind them, a grave contains ashes from the Syonan Chureito, a monument built during the Japanese Occupation to honor Japanese soldiers who died in the taking of Singapore. The Japanese removed the monument at the end of the war for fear it would face desecration and moved the ashes here.

The Japanese Cemetery Park closed to new burials in 1973, and became an official memorial park in 1987. Today the park offers a serene repose, carefully maintained by the Japanese Association, which built a picturesque Prayer Hall in 1986 and replanted a few rubber trees to remember the cemetery's origins.

> The tomb of Field Marshal Count Hisaichi Terauchi, supreme commander of the Southern Command of the Japanese Imperial Army, is also in the cemetery, but it is empty. He died a prisoner of war in Johor in 1946 and his ashes were flown back to his family in Japan.

FIRST POSTWAR FILM STUDIO

A onetime hive of cinematic activity

Singapore Film Studios
8 Jalan Ampas
MRT: Novena

On a quiet side street of nondescript apartment blocks and industrial buildings off Balestier Road sit several concrete structures that are easy to miss behind a locked gate. An elderly caretaker sweeps up around potted plants scattered about in the otherwise abandoned courtyard, a place that was once an important hive of cinematic activity.

As underwhelming as it seems today, the Shaw Brothers' film studio was the epicenter of Singapore's Golden Age of Cinema in the 1950s and '60s, where actors and singers like the iconic P. Ramlee were groomed and rose to prominence. The studio counted among its visitors Hollywood greats such as Ava Gardner and John Wayne. The Shaws equipped their Jalan Ampas studio with the latest recording equipment, even motion picture cameras imported from America. One of the last movies to be made at the studio was *Raja Bersiong*, which despite an outlay 10 times that of an average movie production in Singapore, did not meet with much success. The movie, based on a story that had been written by then Malaysian Prime Minister Tunku Abdul Rahman, also saw the involvement of the Tunku, or children of the ruler.

Today, the gates are occasionally opened for small groups of intrepid explorers who are curious to see what remains of Singapore's first postwar film studio, turning the spotlight once again on what was once such an important stage for the region's beloved movies (Jane's SG Tours offers wonderful film night tours here once or twice a year: www.janestours.sg/). A row of numbered recording rooms is mostly empty now, but vestiges of the old days remain around the property. Along the back of the

building is a "Silence" sign above a peeling wooden door that once flashed red when recording was taking place inside. A large cumbersome camera with giant film reels has been left behind in the courtyard and several SB (Shaw Brothers) logos remain on the building walls.

In the 1930s, the wealthy Shaw Brothers (Run Run and Runme), whose father had made his fortune in the textile trade in Shanghai, got into the film business in Singapore, operating film studios, distribution networks, and theaters. In 1947 they opened Singapore's first postwar film studio, Singapore's "Mollywood" for Malay films. Over two decades, more than 160 films were produced at the Shaw Studios by the brothers' company, Malay Film Productions (MFP), including its first release, the musical comedy *Singapura Di-Waktu Malam*, or *Singapore At Night*. The only other competition in those days was Cathay. Both companies survive today in name with multiplex cinemas around Singapore.

OLD KHONG GUAN BISCUIT FACTORY

A quirky mid-century wedge of a building with an appetizing past

2 MacTaggart Road
MRT: Tai Seng

In an area known for humdrum blocks of warehouses and light manufacturing, an odd building that looks a bit like a boat is hidden in plain sight.

Wedged into the sharp angle where MacTaggart and Burn roads meet, the faded post-war trapezoid-shaped Modernist building has quite an appetizing past. At the very top of its main façade, two large Chinese characters bear the name of one of Singapore's most beloved and successful home-grown brands, Khong Guan, started by two brothers who had immigrated from China.

They built this three-story factory in 1952. The lower floors housed Khong Guan's office, storeroom and a shop, while on upper floors some of the Chew family members resided for a time. Distinct Modernist features make this building shine, from simple decorative trims in colored mosaic tiles to narrow windows framed by vertical fins, porthole-shaped windows and the old-style patterns of the window grilles.

What Singaporean hasn't relished biting the sweet blob of colored sugar icing off a tiny Khong Guan gem biscuit? But how many know that this company at one time held the distinction of being the second-most popular biscuit brand in China? The impressive accolade was bestowed upon the company by consumer brand publication Zhong Guo Ming Pai in 1993.

Not bad for a little company started in the wake of World War II. Chew Choo Keng, a young pre-war immigrant from China's Fujian province, worked at a biscuit factory before striking out on his own, first with a couple of successful ventures in Malaya before settling in Singapore and starting Khong Guan Biscuit Factory with about US$184,000 in capital. His brother, Chew Choo Han, was his close business manager. Together they built a fortune from this and another business, Khong Guan Flour Milling.

While both brothers are deceased, the family still owns the building, which was given conservation status in 2005. The Chew family plans to conserve the building's façade, while updating the interior to accommodate light manufacturing.

KALLANG AIRPORT RUNWAY

A road that was a runway

Old Airport Road
MRT: Mountbatten

Old Airport Road isn't a road that led to the former Kallang Airport, Singapore's first purpose-built airport that operated from 1937 to 1955: the road itself was actually a runway.

Kallang Airport's first runway was a landing strip that the Japanese paved over during the occupation. After the war in 1951-52, the runway was extended. This extension was converted into a road for vehicular traffic when the airport closed in 1955 and today it's still an important artery connecting busy Mountbatten and Tanjong Katong roads.

In the old days, the Kallang Airport, also known as the Kallang Aerodrome, Kallang Airfield and RAF Kallang, had a circular aerodrome

that allowed planes to land from any direction. A slipway in the adjacent Kallang River accommodated seaplanes at the same terminal building as regular planes.

Construction began in 1931 with the reclamation of more than 300 acres of mangrove swamp at the confluence of the Kallang, Geylang and Rochore streams. In its heyday, the Kallang Airport was described as the finest airport in the British Empire. Simple and elegant, the British Modernist beauty was designed by Frank Dorrington Ward, the chief architect of the Public Works Department. The smooth streamline curves and crisp horizontal lines of the glass, steel and concrete two-story terminal and open-air control tower have aged well, thanks in part to a facelift in the 1990s when its green-tinted windows, original main gate, lampposts and tiers of steps at the base of the building were restored. Luckily, the pretty terminal was gazetted for conservation in 2008. After it was decommissioned, the airport was used as the headquarters for the People's Association, part of the government's Ministry of Culture, and later as a venue for events like fashion shows. Its once-vast airfield has been the site of Singapore's national stadiums for decades, including the newest one, a massive 55,000-seater with a retractable roof called the Singapore Sports Hub. The plan at press time was to repurpose Kallang Airport, perhaps as an F&B outlet, to complement the new sports complex.

"An aviation miracle of the East"

Famous aviator Amelia Earhart climbed out of her silver Lockheed Electra after landing it on the grassy runway of Singapore's brand new Kallang Airport in 1937 for a 12-hour stopover during her second around-the-world attempt. As the story goes, Earhart was impressed by the airport next to the Kallang River Basin, calling it "an aviation miracle of the East."

OLD SEAWALLS & STEPS

Seawalls once separated fancy estates
from the nearby beach

Singapore's East Coast
Marine Parade Road
MRT: Mountbatten

A century and more ago, fancy mansions were built along Singapore's east coast, many in the Katong neighborhood, with lawns stretching out to the beach. Before land reclamation began dramatically altering Singapore's shoreline in the 1960s, a seawall was the only thing between the coastal mansions and the water's edge.

A few bits of this seawall still exist along today's Marine Parade Road, which was built close to the original shoreline. Just east of Still Road, you can still spot a section of old stone wall from Colonial times with stairs that once led to the sea, though the mansion it once protected from the ocean is long gone. Another section of seawall can be spotted near the corner of Nallur Road and Marine Parade Road.

A grand seaside estate

One place where you can still spot an old wall and the mansion that it encloses is at the intersection of Still Road and Marine Parade Road. The thick wall stands roughly where the beach would have bordered the Karikal Mahal estate, back when it was built in 1917-1920 by rich Indian cattle merchant Moona Kadir Sultan. At the time, the east coast was a serene place where breezes from the South China Sea kept things cooler, miles from the bustle of crowded downtown Singapore. Kadir's manor cost him about a half million Straits Dollars, a fortune at the time. He went all out, modeling it on a mixture of classic Italianate, Victorian and Indian-inspired architecture, with arches, Corinthian columns, pilasters and ornate plaster moldings. It was large enough for Kadir's numerous wives and brood of children, with four separate houses keeping everyone happy. An artificial lake and fountain were set amid expansive gardens.

After WWII in 1947, Kadir's estate was sold to Lee Rubber Company and turned into the budget 20-room Grand Hotel, a step down for the once opulent compound, but still beloved for its location and easy access to the seashore. The hotel soldiered on until 2000 when it closed. Conservation status was secured in 2003 and in 2016 Lee Rubber rented them out to two pre-schools that restored them beautifully. New beginnings for a grand dame.

TOK LASAM'S GRAVE

Tomb of the legendary founder of Siglap

Field at the end of Jalan Sempadan, off Upper East Coast Road
MRT: Bedok (Siglap MRT to open in 2024)

In an open field, flanked by two great trees, are the tombs of Tok Lasam and his wife. There are at least four versions of the legend of Tok Lasam and his origins and exploits, but they all concur on the fact that he was responsible for the founding of Siglap Village on the east coast of Singapore.

The most implausible of these legends posits that Tok Lasam had come from Sulawesi in the 17th century and died at the age of 162.

The most believable of the many stories, however, was that he was a minor prince – originally named Raja Sufian (Prince Sufian) – from Sumatra in present-day Indonesia. He and his followers had landed somewhere on the east coast of Singapore Island and decided to settle there. In 1821, after witnessing Singapore's only full solar eclipse, Tok Lasam named his village Kampong Siglap, the word being the corruption of "Si-Gelap" meaning a place of darkness. Tok Lasam was said to have married Nai, a lady from Johor who bore him many children.

Pirate whisperer

Tok Lasam was well known for his ability in handling pirates. On one occasion, a ship from China that was carrying smuggled opium anchored at the shore of Siglap. This created a dilemma for the British. Tok Lasam, wearing fisherman clothes, went near the Chinese ship with the excuse of selling his fish. The Captain invited him on board and Tok Lasam persuaded the Captain to surrender and brought him to the police station. Thereafter, the number of pirate activities declined. Tok Lasam did not ask for any recognition from the British. He was then made Penghulu (Headman) of Kampung Siglap.

A check on title deeds showed that in 1860 land in the vicinity of Jalan Sempadan was granted to a Penghulu (Headman) Abdul Assam. It would appear that the name Abdul Assam is a transliteration of Tok Lasam and that they are in fact the same person.

JACKIE CHAN'S ANCIENT CHINESE HOUSES

Unique in Singapore

Singapore University of Design and Technology (SUTD)
8 Somapah Road
MRT: Upper Changi or EXPO

Completed in 2015, the futuristic Singapore University of Design and Technology's (SUTD) campus boasts sleek buildings and landscaping. Designed by Dutch outfit UNStudio and local firm DP Architects, the buildings are brightly-colored and distinct looking. However, what makes a visit to SUTD worth the journey east to Somapah Road is not the new but the old. Mixed into the contemporary complex are four ancient structures that at first glance may seem at odds with the modernity that surrounds them.

Dating back some 400 years, the structures originate from Zhejiang province in China. They are a Chinese opera stage, a Qing-period pavilion and parts of two houses from the Ming and Qing periods. Donated by a most unlikely source (Hong Kong action star Jackie Chan), the structures are the only ones of their kind in Singapore where the traditional Chinese design is Minnan style of southern Fujian.

A feature of the Zhejiang style to look for in the four artifacts is the exquisitely carved, oversized corbels or structural supports. The pavilion is striking for its wooden Suzhou-style balustrades. Look up, above the opera stage, to see the interesting construction of the ceiling: it's shaped like a dome and is a clever way to enhance the acoustics of the open-air stage.

Set over an artificial lake are the front and back portions of two different houses of a similar width. Assembled as if they were one house, the structures are closed by glass panels to permit air-conditioning. The front half would have been where the main hall was located. This was traditionally where guests were received and features fine-finished wooden columns. By contrast, the inner hall in the back, where private areas such as bedrooms would have been, is fitted with coarse unfinished columns, a practice that was prevalent to save costs: out of sight, out of mind.

The donation of the ancient structures in 2009, resulting in the transfer of China's cultural relics out of the country, was not without controversy. Chan, however, felt they could be best preserved in the university. The four are from a set of 10 Chan purchased, dismantled and put into storage in the 1990s with the intention that they be reassembled for use by his parents. Chinese craftsmen had to be enlisted to help assemble the structures, as not much was documented on how they originally had been put together.

RETRO TV TEST PATTERN MURALS

Murals of a TV test pattern on public housing blocks

Public Housing Blocks
Tampines Street 41
MRT: Tampines

Some of Singapore's HDB apartment complexes are painted in bright colors and have funky metal window shades or the giant numbers of their address emblazoned on their facades, but few are covered with giant murals that mean something. If you passed by and happened to look up from your phone, or craned your neck from your seat in a car, taxi or bus, you might notice the retro images stretched across the facades of 15 housing blocks on Tampines Street 41 are more than just abstract decoration.

They're six-story-high images of an old television broadcast test pattern, the very same ones that helped TV stations and viewers fine-tune television reception for focus and color correction, with a variety of different test patterns around the world.

The specific one that appears in these murals, with a set of shapes, lines and colors that formed a circle in a square pattern, was the test pattern employed in Singapore. Older Singaporeans will recognize this pattern instantly from the days before 24-hour programming and digital television. During the early morning and daytime hours, when local TV stations weren't broadcasting shows, they would point a camera at this test pattern and transmit the image.

The murals were added to the blocks in 2015, during routine redevelopment and rejuvenation works, as a way to use social memories to add not only some character to the buildings but as a means to give residents a sense of belonging. At the start of renovations, Tampines Member of Parliament Baey Yam Keng, who had an eye for design, saw a number of proposed color schemes for exterior repainting and remarked that one of the schemes resembled the colors of the old familiar TV test pattern. Eventually, Tampines residents voted for this one and the beloved pattern was painted on the buildings that could structurally accommodate the murals.

OLD CHANGI PRISON GATES ⑭

A symbol of suffering and of the strength
of the human spirit during the war

Upper Changi Road
Bus No. 2 from MRT: Tanah Merah or Bus No. 29 from MRT: Tampines

Today, Changi Prison is a modern 21st-century facility, nothing like the 1936-built correctional facility in which tens of thousands of sick and starving Prisoners of War suffered during the Japanese occupation of Singapore in World War II.

While much of that old prison was demolished in 2004, a careful observer will notice that one section of the old gaol's walls, its famous steel entrance gate and two of its wall-mounted watchtowers remain.

Named as Singapore's 72nd National Monument, the preservation of the 650-foot stretch of Changi Prison's walls and turrets did not come easy. The decision was taken only after intense pressure was mounted by Australian politicians in 2003 when the intention to demolish the old complex was announced. Some 15,000 of Changi's POWs had been Australian, and while the sight of the prison may have evoked painful memories of their time there, it was felt that it was important to keep it as a symbol of the sacrifice and suffering of those who survived and perished, as well as a symbol of the strength of the human spirit. The gate especially has meaning as it was made famous by the many photographs published of it with freed POWs streaming out.

So while only a small portion of the original complex has been kept, it resulted in some level of acceptance and closure among those who lobbied for its retention.

The original Changi Gaol's construction came at the tail end of a huge effort to transform the security forces in Singapore in the face of rapid urbanization and rising crime levels. The effort, which took place in the 1920s to the 1930s, also included the construction of a training facility, new police stations and barracks. The prison, built to house 600, started operations in January 1937, five years before Singapore fell to the Japanese.

"WWII POW paints religious murals alluding to prisoners' plight"

The Changi Museum (closed for renovations until at least late 2020)
1000 Upper Changi Rd North
www.changimuseum.sg
Daily 9:30am–5pm (last admission 4:30pm)
Free
Bus 2 from MRT: Tanah Merah – Opp Changi Chapel Museum stop (97201)
Bus 29 from MRT: Tampines to Changi Chapel Museum stop (97209)

Within the Changi Museum is a set of five frescos painted during the Japanese Occupation, unexpected color in an otherwise drab and abandoned barrack block. Intended as decoration for the humble little attap-roof chapel called St. Luke's in the Changi POW camp, four of the murals depict biblical scenes: the Nativity, Ascension, Crucifixion and Last Supper. A fifth is of St. Luke, the patron of physicians. What is perhaps less known about the murals is that they were used by the artist to show what he had observed around him. In the murals' characters are the faces of his fellow prisoners, and, in the Crucifixion, rags the prisoners wore are shown as loin cloths on the slaves. The murals, now protected, are found in Block 151 in restricted Changi Air Base. However, a replica (projections of the murals) can be seen at the nearby revamped Changi Museum, where the chapel has been recreated.

The work of patient Stanley Warren, the Changi Murals are a haunting reminder of the dark days when the room was a makeshift chapel for a POW hospital. Offering solace and hope to ailing soldiers held in captivity far from their homes and families, they also tell us of the triumph of the human spirit in the face of adversity.

Undertaken over a seven-month period from 1942 to 1943, the work was a remarkable achievement. A large part of the Changi garrison was then a POW camp and Roberts Barracks, where Block 151 was, a POW Hospital. Warren executed the task, one asked of him by the prison chaplain, in between bouts of dysentery and renal disease. With few materials to work with, he used brown camouflage paint, crushed blue billiard chalk and paintbrushes made of human hair. Hearing the strains of Merbecke's arrangement of the Litany being sung in the chapel provided the inspiration. He struggled for two months to complete the Nativity by Christmas 1942. The remaining four took less time and were completed by May 1943.

The chapel would be converted into a store and the murals forgotten. It wasn't until 1958 when three and part of a fourth were rediscovered. Warren's identity was established when a book, *The Churches of Captivity in Malaya*, was found, and within its pages, a description of the chapel. Invited to restore his work, Warren first refused, but later changed his mind, coming back just before Christmas 1963. Further restoration was done in 1982, when the Nativity was found, and in 1988. The mural of St. Luke has not been restored. Its lower part was destroyed when the wall it was on was knocked down. Having lost his sketches, Warren decided to leave it as it was found.

THE JOHORE BATTERY

Trace of a WWII 'Monster Gun'

27 Cosford Road
Bus 29 from MRT: Tampines – Changi Baptist Church Stop (97061)

Cosford Road by the western perimeter of Changi Airport is an area marked by high, barbed wire-topped fences around both the airport and the Singapore Prisons' Abington Centre.

Just in front of the green slat-covered prison fences is the strangest of sights: what seems to be an enormous piece of artillery, accompanied by an odd arrangement of concrete spread across the ground.

While the cannon is a replica, the wartime emplacement it rests on isn't. Along with a network of underground structures, the mount was discovered in 1991 when the correctional facility was being built. The emplacement, belonging to No. 1 Gun, would have been one of three in the area on which the "monster guns" of the Johore Battery were mounted. The 15-inch cannons were the largest caliber guns deployed by the British military for coastal defense and had a range of 21 miles. As with two more guns of the same caliber positioned in the west of the island, the three were placed well inshore – out of sight from the sea.

The labyrinth of discovered tunnels contained passageways, magazines and spaces in which equipment essential to the guns' operation were housed. This included machinery for hydraulic lifts used to feed ammunition. Access to the underground structures is not permitted due to safety concerns, but an idea of how they were laid out can be detected in outlines in the concrete emplacement.

The Johore Battery was named in recognition of the US$470,000 contributed by the Sultan of Johor towards the installation. It was a component of the Changi Fire Command, established in 1938 to protect seaward approaches to the eastern Johor Strait where the British Empire's most important naval base in the Far East was located. The command's other batteries, featuring 6- and 9.2-inch guns, were positioned at Pulau Tekong and Pengerang in southeast Johor.

Commonly believed to have pointed in the wrong direction, the coastal guns were actually effective in preventing the attack from the sea in the south – just what they were intended for. Therefore, Japan used overland routes and attacked instead from the north. Several guns, including two of the Johore Battery's, were in fact fired at targets in the north and west just days before Singapore fell. However, the armor-piercing rounds they were provided with were ineffective against ground forces. Destroyed on the night of February 12, 1942, the obliterated gun's metallic remains were thought to have been sold for scrap after the war. All that remains of these monster guns is the one emplacement and its supporting structures.

CHANGI BEACH MASSACRE MARKER ⑰

Sook Ching massacre: the execution of Chinese men by the thousand

Changi Beach Park, Carpark 2
MRT: Changi Airport

Singapore is full of places that seem perfectly normal to the casual observer, but beneath the surface lurks a grim history. Changi Beach is one of those places. If today families stroll and picnic along sandy beaches amid breezy views of the Johore Straits, some 75 years ago Changi Beach was the site of a mass slaughter. A small marble marker is all that remains to remind of the Sook Ching massacre that took place here in 1942.

Within days of capturing Singapore, World War II Japanese Occupation forces set to work rooting out possible threats to their control. They rounded up ethnic Chinese men of fighting age and sent them to screening centers where the men were subjected to a number of arbitrary tests to determine their loyalty to either Britain or China. The Japanese called this operation *Dai Kensho* ("Great Inspection").

Also referred to as Operation Sook Ching ("purge through cleansing" in Chinese), Chinese men who were suspected of being anti-Japanese were immediately packed into trucks and driven to remote areas where they were executed. These sites included beaches in Changi, Punggol, Katong, Tanah Merah and Blakang Mati (present-day Sentosa).

At Changi Beach, the men were bound by ropes in rows of eight to 12 and instructed to walk in groups towards the sea. As each group approached the shallow water, the Japanese soldiers shot them and then stabbed them with bayonets. British and Australian prisoners of war (POWs) were then forced to dig graves for the men, some of whom were still alive, the POWs later reported.

Nobody knows exactly how many men were executed in the Sook Ching massacres. The Japanese official estimate said 5,000, but it is believed to have been more. A Japanese reporter at the time claimed that the number was as high as 50,000 men.

There are other markers to Sook Ching massacre victims at Punggol Beach, on Sentosa and at Beach Road. The latter is the Civilian War Memorial (aka the "chopstick" memorial) built in 1967 in part with funds given by the Japanese government as compensation for the atrocities committed during their occupation.

TECK SENG'S PLACE

A typical Chinese village house in a gem of a place

Jalan Ubin, Pulau Ubin
www.nparks.gov.sg/ubin
2nd and 4th weekend of the month and public holidays, 10am–2pm
Free
Boat from Changi Village Ferry Terminal to Pulau Ubin Jetty (8-minute walk
from jetty)

The 1970s-built House 363-B, otherwise known as Teck Seng's Place, was the home of sundry shop proprietor Chew Teck Seng. It's typical of a humble Chinese village dwelling. No longer lived in, the brick and wooden house on Pulau Ubin has been preserved and refurnished to serve as a model *kampung* (village) house for the handful of visitors to the island that know about it.

Pulau Ubin, one of Singapore's many out islands and the only one that is still inhabited, is a gem. Lying off the northeastern coast of Singapore, the 15 minutes it takes by boat from Changi Point Ferry Terminal is a journey that will take you several decades back in time to a corner of Singapore that is unlike any other.

A parallel world seems to exist on the island: one of a Singapore that existed before it embarked on a path of rapid modernization. The island plays host to clusters of zinc-roofed wooden houses. Arranged in rustic settings around ponds, green plots and dirt paths, these houses recall the days of the *kampung* – villages in which much of Singapore's rural population was once accommodated. Near the island's village center, Teck Seng's Place is built on an easy-to-clean base of cement. The rooms of the house have generous ventilation openings, a typical feature of tropical house design before fans or air-conditioners came into use. The rooms are spartanly furnished by today's standards and provide a sense of the simplicity of life in the *kampung*. Some common household items include a meat-safe, a foot-pedal sewing machine, dachings (a type of scale commonly used in the shops and markets), and other long-forgotten and obsolete implements.

STATUE OF THE BLESSED VIRGIN MARY

A surprising gift of Sultan Ibrahim of Johor

Church of the Nativity of the Blessed Virgin Mary
1259 Upper Serangoon Road, Singapore 534795

It's of course not surprising to see a statue of the Virgin Mary right in front of the Church of the Nativity of the Blessed Virgin Mary. What is surprising, however, is its origin – it was given by Sultan Ibrahim of Johor in December 1946 as a token of his friendship with Reverend Father Francis Chan (later Bishop of Penang), who was the parish priest of the church from 1946 to 1955.

The marble statue shows Mary standing upon a globe and crushing the head of a serpent under her feet. The Sultan also presented a similar statue of the Blessed Virgin Mary to the Church of Our Lady of Lourdes (now Church of the Immaculate Conception) in Johor.

The link between the two churches is Father Jean Casimir Saleilles, who came to Singapore from Hong Kong on May 23, 1884. He contributed to the construction of this church, and also founded the church in Johor. He passed away in 1916, but the two statues are reminders of his contributions. His tomb can be found in the nave of the church.

Constructed at the turn of the 20th century, and declared open on Dec. 8, 1901, the Church of the Nativity of the Blessed Virgin Mary is one of the earliest Catholic churches built in the suburbs of Singapore. It catered to the Teochew Chinese Catholics living in Upper Serangoon and Punggol at that time. Today, there are Masses in English, Teochew, Mandarin, and Korean.

The architect of this church, Father Charles B. Nain, also designed the former CHIJ Chapel and the curved wings of the former St Joseph's Institution. He was killed in the First World War: his name is one of the 124 inscribed on the Cenotaph.

KAMPONG LORONG BUANGKOK

A hidden kampung dwarfed by residential towers

Off Sengkang East Avenue
MRT: Buangkok

Nestled in a small patch of forest no larger than three football fields, Kampong Lorong Buangkok is a rural village (*kampung* in Malay) dwarfed by surrounding residential towers and modern developments. Unless told the whereabouts of this hidden place, one could breeze right past it. But it's worth the time to seek out, as it is earmarked for redevelopment. Soon it will disappear, taking with it Singapore's last mainland *kampung* and a link to the city-state's humble past.

A must-go for nostalgia buffs, the *kampung* is almost unchanged since its establishment in the mid-1950s. Dirt paths link simple single-family homes with timber walls and corrugated zinc roofs. Roosters crow and chickens cluck while cats pick their way freely among gardens shadowed by tropical foliage and fruit trees. An old *surau* (Muslim place of worship) is managed by a village headman. Even the rents on these

homes have changed little, with residents, virtually all of whom have lived here for decades, paying a mere US$5 to $22 each per month. If they're short of cash, payment in rice or fruit also is accepted.

Their landlady is Sng Mui Hong, the *towkay*, or boss, of the village. Her father Sng, a seller of traditional Chinese medicine, purchased the slightly over three acres of swampy land here in 1956. At the time, it was home to only a handful of families, but soon the swamps were filled in, the houses were built, and up to 40 families called the place home. Despite improvements, the village is still prone to flooding, thus its nickname Kampong Selak Kain, translated as "hitching up the sarong." The father passed away in 1997, leaving the land to Sng and her three siblings. Though they've moved out, she remains to manage the place for the 28 or so remaining Chinese and Malay families.

Estimates place the value of this land at about US$24.5 million. In 2009, Singapore's Urban Redevelopment Authority (URA) announced that the land would be acquired by the state to make way for a major roadway linking Buangkok Drive. The plan has met with some protest, as many Singaporeans don't want to lose this precious connection to their past.

KAYAKING ON SUNGEI KHATIB BONGSU

One of Singapore's last large mangrove forests

Sungei Khatib Bongsu
Off Yishun Avenue 8
kayakasia.org/destinations/

Sungei Khatib Bongsu in Singapore's north is one of the last rivers without a dam built across its mouth: most of Singapore's rivers are dammed as reservoirs for fresh water. It is also one of a handful left with a naturally occurring watery forest that holds one of Singapore's largest concentrations of mangrove trees. An excellent way to see the river and its mangrove forest is by kayak. Trips in groups can be arranged through a water adventure company.

The mangroves feature a collection of trees with long water roots that play host to an amazing collection of fauna. Birds are in abundance, attracted to rich pickings from the mangroves' aquatic nurseries. More than 180 species (half of all bird species found in Singapore) have been recorded. A paddle through the area can often be rewarded with the sighting of a rare or endangered bird such as a great-billed heron or a grey-headed fish eagle.

A maze of channels is found along the river's right bank, a remnant of the once-thriving prawn farming industry that the estuary and several others were home to. Enclosed by manmade bunds of mud, the former prawn pools are interconnected through concrete-lined openings in the bunds that sluice gates had once kept shut. It is possible to kayak through these openings, which are evidence of Singapore's forgotten agricultural past.

Mangrove forests such as Sungei Khatib Bongsu's lined a fair bit of Singapore's coast and around its tidal estuaries, making up as much as 13% of the total land area at modern Singapore's founding in 1819. Many of these salt and brackish water marshes were to be filled and drained over time, starting with those in central Singapore in the area where Boat Quay is now. Today mangrove forests account for only 1% of Singapore's land area.

Ecologically, these forests were important as nurseries for aquatic and marine life, and protected the coastline from erosion. They would have provided both food and safe haven for the native communities of boat dwelling *Orang Laut* (Sea Gypsies), who hung out in the mangroves of the northern coast including Sungei Khatib Bongsu, where the Orang Seletar tribe of Sea Gypsies had lived. The name Seletar was thought to have been derived from the word *selat*, or "strait." While the Sea Gypsy communities of Singapore have largely assimilated into the wider Malay community, there are still small communities of Orang Seletar found just across the strait in Malaysia.

ADMIRALTY HOUSE BOMB SHELTER

A private bomb shelter for a Japanese Admiral

345 Old Nelson Road
Sembawang
www.janestours.sg/
Included on WWII tours of the area (from companies like Jane's Singapore Tours)
MRT: Sembawang or Admiralty

The Old Admiralty House strikes a handsome profile, its stately Arts and Crafts style architecture providing an atmospheric vintage backdrop for an international boarding school that had occupied it recently. Little known to most, however, is the underground bomb shelter on the front lawn that some believe may even be part of a

network of undiscovered tunnels that lead all the way to the old military dockyard at Sembawang.

Built during WWII for a ranking officer, likely a Japanese admiral in the Imperial Japanese Navy living in Admiralty House during the Japanese occupation of Singapore, the bomb shelter is entered by a set of stairs. The 30-square-meter bunker consists of two small rooms that were fitted with lighting and an Asian-style squatting toilet. The British government in Singapore built few bomb shelters of their own during the war because they didn't want to upset the locals, preferring to downplay the threat of invasion.

After the war, the entrance was closed and covered by foliage. In the 1990s, the bunker was re-discovered after a mini-excavator sunk into the ground during routine landscape work, revealing what was underneath.

The 1940-built house served as the residence for the Commodore Superintendent of the Royal Navy Dockyard and changed names several times. The British Royal Navy called it Canberra House until after World War II, when it was renamed Nelson House. For a brief moment in the 1970s, it was known as ANZUK House, for the combined forces (Australia, New Zealand, UK) that provided military defense at the time. It was officially gazetted as a national monument and called Old Admiralty House in 2002.

Sembawang: the biggest naval dock in the world

The Sembawang area gets its name from the tall Sembawang trees in the area. Before colonial settlers arrived, *orang seletar*, indigenous nomadic sea-dwellers, lived in their boats here. The area was first cleared for gambier and pepper plantations in the 1800s, which shifted to rubber and pineapple in the early 1900s.

In the 1920s, the Royal British Navy established a base from Sembawang Road to the Causeway in Woodlands, that included barracks, workshops, hospitals and airbases. In 1938, with the official opening of the graving dock, or dry dock, Sembawang was the biggest naval dock in the world, earning it the moniker "Gibralter of the East."

In 1968, as the British began the withdrawal of their troops, the Royal British Navy sold the base to the Singapore government for a token sum of $1. Today, the shipyard is known as Sembcorp Marine, part of Sembcorp Industries, a government-linked commercial entity with shipyards around the world.

BEAULIEU HOUSE

Last patch of natural beach

117 Beaulieu Road
Sembawang Park
MRT: Admiral

With a lovely view overlooking the Straits of Johor, the Neoclassical Beaulieu House was built in the 1910s during a time when seaside retreats were all the rage. Because land reclamation over the decades has transformed so much of Singapore's coastline, it is believed the stretch of beach at Beaulieu House may be the last remaining patch of natural beach.

A century ago, the most favorable sites for waterfront mansions were the beaches that lined Katong and Pasir Panjang. However, massive land

reclamation projects in each of those areas has rendered Beaulieu House the only retreat still located at the seaside.

In front of the house, the jetty and a rare stretch of natural sand beach are part of Sembawang Park. Here, birdwatchers have spotted eagles, kites, kingfishers and orioles. The pathways around the park have been restored from their creation during the British military days.

With its distinctive sloping roof topped by a patio surrounded by decorative cast-iron balustrades, the Beaulieu bungalow is believed to have been built by a Jewish family named David, the head of which ran mines in Malaya and was involved in horse racing and real estate ventures in Singapore. A decade after the house was built, the British Royal Navy began building its naval base nearby, and subsequently purchased the house and around 1,730 acres of land surrounding it for US$77,600. It became the residence for senior engineers during the construction of the base, and later housed officers.

Beaulieu House was granted conservation status in 2005, and today houses a restaurant that takes advantage of the mansion's high ceilings and vintage decorative elements such as patterned tile floors and ornate wall plaster.

In French, *beau lieu* means "beautiful place."

ALPHABETICAL INDEX

Admiralty House bomb shelter	248
"An aviation miracle of the East"	221
Anna and the King of Siam	63
Another POW mural	153
Arrows on bricks	142
Aw brothers	27
Baby Gate or the Gate of Hope	92
Basketball-themed window grills	16
Beaulieu House	250
Beginning of the end	157
Black and white houses at Mount Pleasant Road	208
Block 53 Toa Payoh's Y shape	214
Boardroom at the former Ford Factory	168
Bronze thai elephant	62
Buildings of Middle Road's early communities	110
Building of the Year 2018	161
Bukit brown peacock tiles	212
Bukit Timah Summit	168
Cavaliere Rodolfo Nolli	67
Changi Beach massacre marker	236
Chee Guan Chiang house	104
City Hall Chamber	64
Civilian pre-war air-raid shelter	42
Clan associations and schools	103
Colonnade	106
Communal Riots of 1964	135
Conservation Victory	115
Drinking fountain at the National Museum of Singapore	86
Dutch Windmill on a Chinese Grave	213
Duxton Plain Park	28
Early Founders' Stone	50
Ellison Building's cupolas	114
Ex Malayan Motors showroom	96
Faces of Changi murals	232
Factory years	169
Façade of 66 Spottiswoode Park Road	32
First mosque in Singapore to be named after a woman	133
First postwar film studio	216
Flagpole of "Eden Hall"	146
Foot of the Sir Stamford Raffles statue	58
For a better view	169
Forbidden Hill	79
Former brewmaster's house	186
Fort Canning Lighthouse	70
Fort Canning's tombstone wall	78
Fort Imbiah Battery	196
Freemasons Hall	72
From bread seller to stockbroker	95
From fruit hawker to hospital builder	45
Fullerton Hotel Heritage Gallery	48
Fullerton Hotel lighthouse beacon	188
Gap	180
Garden of Fame	174
Gasholder frame	134
Gate pillars of Nan Chiau High School	102
Girl on A Swing sculpture	144
Goddess Kali with a bite	118
Grand Seaside Estate	223
Gravestone of the first person born in Colonial Singapore	79
Grisly finds under Anderson Bridge	53
Harbourfront 19th-century steam crane	194
Hexagonal pavilion of the Tiger Balm pagoda	26
Hidden tomb	29
Holiday apartment used by late Dr Goh Keng Swee	203
Istana Woodneuk	138
Jackie Chan's ancient Chinese houses	226
Jalan Kubor cemetery	126
James Cutler mail chute	12
Japanese Cemetery Park	215
Jewish traders in Singapore	99
John Gemmill and the Gemmill Lane	87
Johore Battery	234
Kallang Airport runway	220
Kampong Kapoor	119
Kampong Lorong Buangkok	242
Kampung Admiralty rooftop	160
Kayaking on Sungei Khatib Bongsu River	246
Leaning minaret of Hajjah Fatimah Mosque	132
Library of Botany and Horticulture	140
Lions on the Elgin Bridge	66
Little Guilin	170
Longest continuous sky gardens in the world	25
Lost hills of Singapore	23
Lost islands of Singapore	22
Mace of Singapore	80
Machine-gun pillbox	176
Malay lexicon	23
Manasseh Meyer's initials	98

Meeting of the Overseas Chinese Association 17

Memorial and shrine to Sikh martyr Bhai Maharaj Singh 34

Memorial to James Brooke Napier 76

Mount Emily swimming complex: Singapore's oldest public pool 69

Nantah Arch 172

Neil Road: a hero of the 1857 Indian Mutiny 31

Night soil vents 120

Not exactly Art Deco 43

NUS Baba House 30

Old Changi prison gates 230

Old Khong Guan biscuit factory 218

Old library gate pillars 88

Old school 207

Old seawalls 222

One-Two-Six Cairnhill Arts Centre 206

Organ of the Cathedral of the Good Shepherd 90

Origin of Petain Road 117

Original gate to "The New World" amusement park 122

Original steps to Haw Par Villa 178

Other secret details 41

Part of the Royal Malaysian Navy until 1997 159

Paul Revere Bell 82

Paul Revere: famous for more than bells 83

Paul Rudolph: one of the great architects of the late-modern period 107

Petain Road Townhouse 124

Phantom pool 68

Pier at Lim Chu Kang 156

Pillboxes 177

Pirate whisperer 225

Plantation Nation: Burkill Hall 140

Plaque of Alexandra Hospital 184

Plaque of Anderson Bridge 52

Pre-World War II Japanese community at Middle Road 111

Profit-making gardens 151

Pulau Blakang Mati: once a bastion of military might 197

Raffles Lighthouse 202

Remains of Stamford Bridge 56

Retro TV test pattern murals 228

Rubber-Obsessed Ridley 149

Sarkies phantom tombs 74

Secrets of the "home" mural 40

Sembawang Hot Springs 162

Sembawang: The Biggest Naval Dock in the World 249

Sentosa boardwalk 198

Shophouse 33

Shophouse at No. 1 Tank Road 100

Sikh tomb guardians of Bukit Brown Cemetery 210

Singapore Botanic Garden's tiger orchid 141

Singapore City Gallery 18

Singapore General Hospital Museum 38

Singapore land indentures 20

Singapore stone 84

Singapore's highest building 25

Singapore's land reclamation story 22

Singapore's oldest lift 21

Soy sauce bottle bottoms of the Sultan Mosque 130

Stained glass windows at Jacob Ballas Centre 94

Star hexagram: a magical talisman? 112

Statue of the Blessed Virgin Mary 240

Straits settlements police crest 14

Stump-ument to Singapore's first rubber tree 148

Sunburst of Masjid Abdul Gaffoor 116

Symbolism of Nantah Arch 173

Syonan Jinja shrine 164

Tan Kim Seng Fountain 54

Tan Tock Seng's tombstone 44

Tanah Kubur Diraja 36

Teck Seng's place 238

'Toilet Water' 163

Tok Lasam's grave 224

Towers of lights seen from Ghost Island 200

Tree Tapping Genius 149

Tudor Rose 60

View from Pinnacle@Duxton 24

Wartime Japanese grave 192

Where the surrender of the Japanese forces took place 65

White obelisk at Labrador Park 190

Wooden arrow 150

Woodlands jetty 158

World's tallest public housing building 25

WWII POW calendar 152

Ying Fo Fui Kun cemetery 182

Zubir Said's piano 128

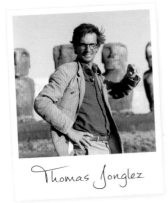

Thomas Jonglez

It was September 1995 and Thomas Jonglez was in Peshawar, the northern Pakistani city 20 kilometres from the tribal zone he was to visit a few days later. It occurred to him that he should record the hidden aspects of his native city, Paris, which he knew so well. During his seven-month trip back home from Beijing, the countries he crossed took in Tibet (entering clandestinely, hidden under blankets in an overnight bus), Iran and Kurdistan. He never took a plane but travelled by boat, train or bus, hitchhiking, cycling, on horseback or on foot, reaching Paris just in time to celebrate Christmas with the family.

On his return, he spent two fantastic years wandering the streets of the capital to gather material for his first "secret guide", written with a friend. For the next seven years he worked in the steel industry until the passion for discovery overtook him. He launched Jonglez Publishing in 2003 and moved to Venice three years later.

In 2013, in search of new adventures, the family left Venice and spent six months travelling to Brazil, via North Korea, Micronesia, the Solomon Islands, Easter Island, Peru and Bolivia. After seven years in Rio de Janeiro, he now lives in Berlin with his wife and three children. Jonglez Publishing produces a range of titles in nine languages, released in 30 countries.

FROM THE SAME PUBLISHER

PHOTO BOOKS

Abandoned America
Abandoned Asylums
Abandoned Australia
Abandoned churches – Unclaimed places of worship
Abandoned cinemas of the world
Abandoned France
Abandoned Italy
Abandoned Japan
Abandoned Spain
After the Final Curtain – The Fall of the American Movie Theater
After the FInal Curtain – America's Abandoned Theaters
Baikonur – Vestiges of the Soviet space programme
Forbidden Places – Exploring our Abandoned Heritage Vol. 1
Forbidden Places – Exploring our Abandoned Heritage Vol. 2
Forbidden Places – Exploring our Abandoned Heritage Vol. 3
Forgotten Heritage
Unusual wines
Venice deserted

'SECRET' GUIDES

New York: Hidden bars & restaurants
Secret Amsterdam
Secret Bali – An unusual guide
Secret Barcelona
Secret Belfast
Secret Berlin
Secret Brighton – An unusual guide
Secret Brooklyn
Secret Brussels
Secret Buenos Aires
Secret Campania
Secret Cape Town
Secret Copenhagen
Secret Dublin – An unusual guide
Secret Edinburgh – An unusual guide
Secret Florence
Secret French Riviera
Secret Geneva
Secret Granada
Secret Helsinki
Secret Istanbul
Secret Johannesburg
Secret Lisbon
Secret Liverpool – An unusual guide
Secret London – An unusual guide
Secret London – Unusual bars & restaurants
Secret Los Angeles
Secret Madrid
Secret Mexico City
Secret Milan
Secret Montreal – An unusual guide
Secret Naples
Secret New Orleans
Secret New York – An unusual guide
Secret New York – Curious activities
Secret Paris
Secret Prague
Secret Provence
Secret Rio
Secret Rome
Secret Sussex
Secret Tokyo
Secret Tuscany
Secret Venice
Secret Vienna
Secret Washington D.C.
Secret York

'SOUL OF' GUIDES

Soul of Athens – A guide to 30 exceptional experiences
Soul of Barcelona – A guide to 30 exceptional experiences
Soul of Lisbon – A guide to 30 exceptional experiences
Soul of Los Angeles – A guide to 30 exceptional experiences
Soul of New York – A guide to 30 exceptional experiences
Soul of Rome – A guide to 30 exceptional experiences
Soul of Tokyo – A guide to 30 exceptional experiences
Soul of Venice – A guide to 30 exceptional experiences

Follow us on Facebook, Instagram and Twitter

...ho have inspired me and fed my ...ith special gratitude to co-author ...ave explored with me, especially ...ations and chart the book's maps, ...d joined me in a bushwhacking ...d for her ace editing and writing ...; me when I droned on about my ...Kevin YL Tan, president of the Singapore Heritage Society, for contributing 10 secrets to the book at the onset; to artist and "Singapore Heritage Tiles: An International Mosaic of Love" author Jennifer Lim for insights and photos of ceramic tiles in Bukit Brown; and to tour guides Geraldene Lowe-Ishmael and Jane Iyer, for stoking my passion for Singapore's secret side.

Jerome Lim
I wish to offer my thanks to Heidi Sarna for the opportunity to do this and also for her patience, as well as the many friends who have encouraged me on what started as a personal journey some ten years back to uncover that side of Singapore that is all too often overlooked.

Thomas Jonglez
Jean-Luc Boucharenc, Christian Boucharenc.

ADDITIONAL CONTRIBUTION
Sarah Teo Joo: The Plaque of Anderson Bridge; Remains of Stamford Bridge; Drinking Fountain at the National Museum of Singapore; Statue of the Blessed Virgin Mary; Ying Fo Fui Kun Cemetery.

PHOTOGRAPHY CREDITS
All photos are by **Heidi Sarna** except these:
Chapter 1 – *James Cutler Mail Chute*, Jerome Lim; *Basketball-Themed Window Grills*, Jerome Lim & Robin McAdoo; *Singapore's Oldest Lift*, Jerome Lim; *Land Reclamation Map*, Robin McAdoo; *Duxton Plain Park*, Jerome Lim; *NUS Baba House Museum*, NUS Baba House; *Singapore's Oldest Surviving Façade*, Jerome Lim; *Tanah Kubor Diraja*, Jerome Lim; *Civilian Pre-War Air-Raid Shelter*, Jerome Lim; *Tan Tock Seng's Tombstone*, Jerome Lim.
Chapter 2 – *Early Founder's Stone*, Jerome Lim; *Piece of Egypt on Anderson Bridge*, Sarah Teo; *Tan Kim Seng Fountain*, Jerome Lim; *Remains of Stamford Bridge*, Sarah Teo; *Foot of Sir Stamford Raffles Statue*, Jerome Lim; *Tudor Rose*, Jerome Lim; *City Hall Chamber*, Jerome Lim; *Lions on Elgin Bridge*, Jerome Lim; *Phantom Swimming Pool (water in pool photo)*, Yee Chao Koh; *Fort Canning Lighthouse*, Jerome Lim; *Freemasons Hall (stained glass photo)*, Catalina Tong; *The Mace of Singapore*, Jerome Lim; *Paul Revere Bell*, National Museum of Singapore; *The Singapore Stone*, Jerome Lim; *Organ of the Cathedral of the Good Shepherd*, Jerome Lim; *Stained Glass Windows at Jacob Ballas Centre*, Jerome Lim; *Chee Guan Chiang House*, Jerome Lim; *Ex Malayan Motors Showroom*, Jerome Lim; *Ex Malayan Motors showroom (smaller photo)*, Henry Cordeiro.
Chapter 3 – *Buildings of Middle Road*, Jerome Lim; *Night Soil Vents*, Jerome Lim; *Zubir Said's Piano*, Jerome Lim.
Chapter 4 – *Singapore Botanic Gardens' Tiger Orchid*, Edmund Chia for NParks; *Arrows on Bricks (Kwan Koriba photo)*, NParks; *Girl on a Swing*, Jerome Lim; *Singapore's First Rubber Tree (black and white photos)*, NParks; *Wooden Arrow (black & white photo)*, NParks; *WWII POW Calendar*, Jon Cooper; *Bukit Brown Peacock Tiles*, Jennifer Lim, author of "Singapore Heritage Tiles: An International Mosaic of Love."
Chapter 5 – *Pier at Lim Chu Kang*, Jerome Lim; *Woodlands Jetty*, Jerome Lim; *Sembawang Hot Springs*, Nparks; *Bukit Timah Summit*, NParks; *Garden of Fame*, Jerome Lim; *Ying Fo Fui Kun Cemetery*, Sarah Teo; *Wartime Japanese Grave*, Jung Kwok; *Towers of Light Seen from Ghost Island*, Jerome Lim; *Raffles Lighthouse*, Jerome Lim.
Chapter 6 – *Block 53 Toa Payoh's Y Shape*, Jerome Lim; *First Postwar Film Studio (black & white photo)*, The Shaw Organisation Pte Ltd; *Kallang Airport Runway (black & white photo)*, Australian War Memorial; *Super Trees Solar Panels*, Gardens by the Bay; *Tok Lasam's Grave*, Jerome Lim; *Jackie Chan's Ancient Chinese Houses*, Jerome Lim; *Old Changi Prison Gates (black & white photo)*, Australian War Memorial; *Faces of Changi Murals*, Jerome Lim; *Johore Battery*, Jerome Lim; *Teck Seng's Place*, Jerome Lim & Nparks (interior photo); *Statue of Blessed Virgin Mary*, Jerome Lim; *Kampong Lorong Buangkok*, Paula Mary Day; *Kayaking on Sungei Khatib Bongsu River*, Jerome Lim.

Cartography: Cyrille Suss – **Design:** Emmanuelle Willard Toulemonde – **Editing:** Sue Pollack – **Proofreading:** Kimberly Bess – **Publishing:** Clémence Mathé

In accordance with regularly upheld French jurisprudence (Toulouse 14-01-1887), the publisher will not be deemed responsible for any involuntary errors or omissions that may subsist in this guide despite our diligence and verifications by the editorial staff.
Any reproduction of the content, or part of the content, of this book by whatever means is forbidden without prior authorisation by the publisher.

© JONGLEZ 2021
Registration of copyright: April 2021 – Edition: 01
ISBN: 978-2-36195-326-3
Printed in Bulgaria by Dedrax